TRACKERS

TRACKERS

The untold story of Australian dogs of war

PETER HARAN

NEW
HOLLAND

First published in 2000 by New Holland Publishers Pty Ltd
Reprinted 2000, 2001, 2013, 2018
London • Sydney • Auckland

131–151 Great Titchfield Street, London WIW 5BB, United Kingdom
1/66 Gibbes Street, Chatswood, NSW 2067, Australia
5/39 Woodside Ave, Northcote, Auckland 0627, New Zealand

newhollandpublishers.com

National Library of Australia Cataloguing-in-Publication Data:

Haran, Peter, 1948–
Trackers: the untold story of the Australian dogs of war.

ISBN 9781864366051

Haran, Peter, 1948–. 2. Vietnamese Conflict, 1962–1975 – Australia
Soldiers – Australia – Biography. 4. Dogs – War use. I. Title.
II. Untold story of the Australian dogs of war.

959.70434

Designer: Kimberley Pearce
Production Director: James Mills-Hicks
Printer: Hang Tai Printing Company Limited

10 9 8 7 6 5 4

Keep up with New Holland Publishers on Facebook
facebook.com/NewHollandPublishers

CONTENTS

ACKNOWLEDGEMENTS

This book was written for two purposes. First, I have tried to provide a snapshot of how life was for the infantry soldier in the Vietnam War; the life of the grunt told via this small piece of reality, as opposed to the dry analysis and 'official' histories which tell little of the war as seen from ground zero.

The second objective was to show how the tracking dogs, and teams, served in Vietnam. I have taken licence with real conversation at times, but have tried to meld the actual spoken word with the need to retain some degree of fluency.

I contacted many former trackers to confirm events and times. Some confirmed events, while others disagreed with my perspective. Many ex-trackers had just vanished or changed their addresses and phone numbers so much I gave up.

However, since the first publication of this book in April 2000, many former dog handlers have contacted me from all over Australia. They have told me stories of their own from the war—enough to fill another book. One of the most memorable—and tearful—pieces of information came from the son of a soldier whose father took over Caesar during the war. 'My dad died in an accident after he came home,' the young man wrote. 'We never really knew what he did in Vietnam. Reading your book, I felt like my father was speaking to me.' Then there was the sister of my friend Gary Polglase, killed in Vietnam, who said, 'I never knew my brother, I was about three when he died. Having read your book, I now feel I know my brother and what he did as a tracker.'

I must also tell you that since *Trackers* was released, I have received news of Caesar from the man who became his owner when he was finally pensioned—at the Australian, not the British Embassy, as I'd previously thought. He wrote: 'Peter, Caesar went to a good home at the Australian Embassy in Saigon in July 1970. In fact, he came to my family and I. We treated him like the war hero he was. He gave hours of enjoyment to my children. He sat in the bathroom and watched me shave—a real man's dog!—and we even took him surfing near Vung Tau. His last years were spent in a home where he was loved.'

I thank Bob and Donny for clarifying aspects of the fire trail fight and Operation Coburg fight. Chris O'Neil from 7RAR Trackers gave a lot of help, as did Mick Fincham of 4RAR and Allyn McCulloch, Vietnam veteran and one of the Army's original dog handlers in Malaya. Les McNicol, ex-3RAR, a trained dog handler who became a forward scout in Vietnam, was always ready to help, and I thank 'Bluey' Bower for his help and description of Nui Dat after his 1997 visit to Vietnam. Bill Fogarty of 7RAR did an archival check in Canberra on the tracking dogs, and Kevin Kanny researched the tracking dogs' disposal at Central Army Records Office.

Former tracking dog handlers who offered help included Rod Purcell, Bobby Bye, Wally Barnett, Bob Pearson and John Parcell. Other trackers who recalled events were Ron 'Tex' O'Toole, Kingsley Paul, Ernie Baxter, Simon Whitehead and Peter Jay. Thanks too Hans Van Zwol, Captain Paul Hampten, Warren Featherby, Jock Statton, Graham Parkes, John Sullivan, Colin Sinclair, Brian Budden and Brian Webber. Thanks to Nick Griffith for his support and motivation.

This book would not have been possible without the enthusiasm of the people at New Holland. That includes Publishing Manager, Anouska Good, who said, 'Let's do it', book editor, Narelle Walford, and project coordinator, Sean Doyle, who fought a deadline—as well as all my old battles—to achieve a quality product.

Peter Haran
Adelaide, June 2000.

FOREWORD

When asked by Peter Haran to write the Foreword for his book, I was initially somewhat apprehensive. You have to remember that the events described in this book occurred over 30 years ago. But once I commenced my own journey down memory lane, those events of the mid-1960s were still so clear in my mind.

I was one of the first young officers to be given the privilege of taking a tracking team into the Vietnam theatre of war. Tracking the enemy, using dogs specifically trained for such a task—alongside soldiers highly trained in recognising tracks—is truly an art. It was proven during the Vietnam conflict that soldiers with the right ingredients of dedication, concentration and bushcraft could become highly trained in recognising and following the spoor left by a quarry.

It was at the onset of Australia's involvement in the Vietnam conflict during the early 1960s that the Australian Army's emphasis of training changed from the conventional style of warfare to jungle or guerilla warfare. The British had used tracking teams with some measure of success during the Malayan Emergency, and it was decided that with Australia's involvement in Vietnam becoming evident, the use of tracking teams would be a useful additional weapon against the enemy. The first Australian tracking dogs were trained in South Australia by Commonwealth Police Officer Mason Clark at the Salisbury dog kennels. The Tracking Wing was established within the School of Infantry at Ingleburn, a small military base on the outskirts of Sydney, and dog training began there in 1966.

Very little has been written about the small group of dedicated soldiers and the tracking dogs that made up the tracking teams assigned to each infantry battalion embarking on their tour of South Vietnam from 1967 onwards. Using tracking teams in an operational environment was a unique experience for the Australians, and in many cases new rules had to be made up as they went along. These tracking teams rarely worked as a full-sized unit, but were usually split into smaller tracking groups consisting of approximately five men. It was these small teams that often had to be winched by helicopter into an operational situation after contact with the enemy had been made by infantry units.

These men, with their tracker dog, had the task of locating the track of a fleeing enemy and following it. Of course, this meant that the small tracking team would lead actual fighting elements towards the enemy—one of the most dangerous jobs in any war. This required both excellent scouting skills from team members as well as absolute confidence in the ability of the tracker dog to be able to 'sense' the enemy before actual contact was made. In addition, the handler had to be able to immediately interpret any changes in the tracker dog's demeanour—after all, men's lives depended on it. The development of very close and strong bonds as a result of working in such small groups, often in very dangerous or potentially dangerous situations, was inevitable.

A key element within the tracking team was of course the tracker dogs. These animals, always black male labrador or labrador crossbreeds, were named after famous Roman emperors; hence you'll see those names featuring throughout the book. Some very fine dogs graduated from that establishment, but in my mind there never was a better dog than one of the two that was allocated to my tracking team and worked with us in South Vietnam. That dog's name was Caesar. Caesar was certainly not the prettiest dog I ever saw, but he was by far the best tracker dog ever trained at the School of Infantry. The other dog that was part of our team was Marcus, a purebred labrador. Whilst not as highly skilled overall as Caesar—and here I must point out that I've never seen any other dog with Caesar's abilities—Marcus was a very fine tracker dog with a big heart and a very gentle nature. He would never give up.

I have never seen a stronger bond develop between humans and animals than I saw with the handlers and their dogs. It is a credit to each of the handlers that the dogs' highly honed skills were retained and that they weren't pampered or spoilt—the dogs had a job to do, and the handlers recognised that.

Because of quarantine laws, these dogs were not allowed to be brought back to Australia, which—while being painful for the tracking team as a whole—was particularly hard to take for each individual handler. I know that many a handler has shed more than one tear for having to leave his dog behind when the unit returned to Australia. As returning to Australia was not an option, it was decided to continue to employ each dog and allocate them to successive tracking teams arriving in South Vietnam until the dog's tracking skills became somewhat diminished, for whatever reason.

On my return from South Vietnam I was given command of the Tracking Wing at the School of Infantry. I was fortunate to meet most of the people that are mentioned in this book, and each one has had his own impact on the short history of tracking teams within the Australian Army. I worked with some exceptionally fine non-commissioned officers and soldiers, both Regular Army and National Servicemen.

Following the end of our involvement in South Vietnam, the Australian Army again reverted to operating on a conventional warfare basis; hence the Tracking Wing was disbanded. A short but exciting chapter in Australia's military history had been closed. The organisation served its purpose well during our involvement in South Vietnam, and it should be with pride that we acknowledge those that served with the tracker teams.

When soldiers go to war, dogs still go, too: today the military uses more dogs than at the height of the Vietnam conflict. The canines have been employed in such specialised fields as mine detection, where Australian-trained dogs work with AUSTCARE in mine clearance overseas; and guard dogs are used for Army and Air Force base protection.

At the time of writing, eight dogs are deployed in East Timor with the Australian Defence Force. The dogs, predominantly German shepherds, are part of the RAAF contingent. They are being used for the defence of Dili Airport, in scouting patrolling roles, and to search for displaced persons. The dogs are working on a rotation system, returning to Australia while others are flown up to the conflict zone.

In this book, Peter Haran has produced a comprehensive account of the history of the tracking team. Whilst *Trackers* serves as an important record of the teams' very short life, it is the human perspective that makes this book such enjoyable reading.

Major (ret.) Leo Van de Kamp
Queensland.

PHUOC TUY PROVINCE

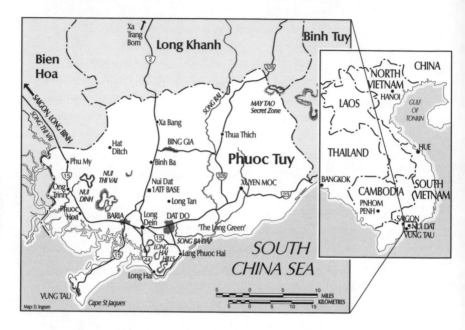

Phuoc Tuy province, known as the 'rice bowl' of South Vietnam, was the only region that was the total responsibility of the Australians during the Vietnam War. The huge American complexes at Bien Hoa and Long Binh (not on map) were north-west of Phuoc Tuy in Bien Hoa province, close to Saigon. In 1965, before 1ATF was established, 1RAR was based at Bien Hoa. In 1967 the Australian Task Force began combined operations outside Phuoc Tuy, in Long Kanh and Bien Hoa.

MEASUREMENTS

The measurements in this book are imperial, in accordance with the practice in Australia in 1967-68. The sole exception to this is the measurement of land distances in Vietnam, which is in kilometres, in accordance with the maps used there by the Australian Army.

Note: 1 mile = 1.61 kilometres

In The Beginning

In early 1966 two officers from the Infantry Training Centre at Ingleburn visited a Sydney dogs' home. They were looking for the lost, the unwanted; those on death row. Specifically, they were keen to examine black labradors, or labrador-crosses, for a new Army project. The dogs needed to be healthy, with no obvious physical impairment, and just a year or two old.

Both men found their attention drawn to one mongrel. He was a labrador–kelpie mix. He looked fit and strong, with one ear that sat erect and one that hung down at a half lop, as if a piece may have been torn out of it in a fight. The Army men noticed the dog also seemed in a state of permanent hyperactivity, paws up against the arcmesh of the cage, tongue lolling out to one side. They figured the dog's eagerness to be noticed may have had something to do with the fact he was only six kennels short of the execution room. The dog had every reason in the world to want out. After a few minutes' discussion they paid $3 to the kennel master, slipped a choker chain around the dog's neck and put him into the back of the Land Rover.

GOING BACK

I was dragged through the Vietnam War on the end of a 20-foot dog leash. Some combatants packed a butt-busting backpack, rifle and bandoliers of ammunition. Others loaded shells into 105 howitzers, or lugged explosives and blew up enemy bunkers. Troopers grunted inside steel-hulled armoured personnel carriers (APCs) and tanks, some fretted over maps figuring where Charlie would be this time tomorrow. Special Air Service (SAS) super-soldiers stalked through the forest on a ghost-who-walks mission looking for the Viet Cong. Then there was me. I was pulled through the bush at the end of a tracking lead.

I was a dog handler in a combat tracking team who spent the war watching a dog's rear end bobbing ahead of me. My life depended on a wet nose and the uncanny animal instinct of a black labrador–kelpie cross smart arse called Caesar.

This tracking dog thought he had the wood on any digger. He did. He could see, smell and hear Charlie long before we walked into a firefight. He knew where the mines were, where the trip wires were strung, and he could cover ground chasing the enemy at speeds which literally took your breath away. He had the shit scared out of him by the odd big bang. That was when he wasn't scaring the shit out of us.

War was a ball for Caesar; the ultimate game for the mongrel who once called a Sydney dog refuge his home.

When I went to Vietnam with Caesar I cursed the day I volunteered to become a tracking dog handler. The day I left him there broke my heart.

Somewhere in the middle of an old rubber plantation in South Vietnam are the remains of two blocks of dog kennels. Those who have been there in recent years say nothing remains of the First Australian Task Force Base (1ATF Base) in Phuoc Tuy province. That's understandable—it has been more than 30 years since 6000 men and machines stirred up choking red dust and created rivers of mud at a place called Nui Dat.

The tent city stood among the tall rubber. It was a place of a million sandbags, artillery pieces thundering during a night mission—where ghosts of Australian soldiers drifted through six years of combat at the 1ATF. For those men during the years 1966 to 1972, Nui Dat was home for their 12-month tour; a chunk of Australia, a self-contained colony wrapped in barbed wire.

The Vietnamese are back there now. Small huts and children, most of whom would never have heard of the *Uc Da Loi*, the people from the Southern Land.

For many, the Vietnam War is a re-run in black-and-white, like the old photos at home in a battered album not often opened. Then I remember the kennels.

The 1ATF Base has been taken back by the bush and the people. Faded, rusted and dismantled. The big rubber trees have been felled and cleared, along with the perimeter wire and the bitumen airstrip of Luscombe Field. But perhaps the concrete kennel floors are still there, under the ferns and leaves. For me, finding them would be like wiping the debris off an old grave.

When the engineers built the kennels in 1967 they were strong timber uprights, with iron roofs and arcmesh along the dog runs. One of the kennels was sandbagged. They were situated in the gentle mottled shade of Nui Dat rubber, almost the sort of place you'd like to take the family dog for a run and roll.

The kennels were home to the war dogs, members of the Australian Military Forces and, like the beat and buggered diggers, they didn't spend much time in the 'Dat during their years of war service.

At the end of 1972, when the last of the soldiers boarded the Chinooks for the final flight out of the war zone, the Australian war dogs were left behind. They had been pensioned off, 'donated' to civilians still serving in South Vietnam. One had died on duty. Naturally they are all now long dead, and I hope they passed on before the country fell to the North Vietnamese in 1975. I suppose the passage of time makes the fact they were abandoned a bit more comfortable for those who knew them.

When I joined the Australian Army in January 1966, I was given a number. Every ex-serviceman remembers his number—it may just as well been barcoded, along with a use-by date, on his forehead. Until the day they nail down the box and drop the old digger in the hole, he'll remember that number. Mine was 43952. Those five digits revealed that I came from South Australia, that I was a Regular Army enlistee, as opposed to a National Serviceman, and that I'd signed on for six years.

And six years is a bloody long time, particularly when you consider that the Australian Army in the 1960s was caught in a time that saw the military shaken from peace activities into a shadowy conflict which rapidly escalated into a political and military wildfire. So it came to pass that during my six years in uniform I was to spend nearly two of them in a South-East Asian backwater that most Australians in 1966 related to Mars, or an image glimpsed on a poster with coolie hats and water buffalos.

It was by becoming 43952 that brought me, 20 years later,

to the large smoke-filled loungeroom of the Phoenician Club in Sydney. There, late one afternoon, I stood wobbling drunk along with dozens of other men with numbers who had also done their time in 'Nam.

I was drinking with veterans from the 2nd Battalion, and our heads were still spinning after a highly emotional, unexpected event called The Welcome Home Parade. In effect it was the country's official Big Sorry Day for the Vietnam veterans who had been head-kicked since they returned from the war; it was a personal purging of demons for many of the 26 000 who had just strode, hobbled or been wheelchaired through the Sydney streets. Although it was 20 years coming, it was definitely therapeutic. Particuarly the post-Parade piss-up.

Saturday, 3 October 1987, and I was falling down drunk. I still cannot clearly recall how or precisely what happened, but suddenly I felt a gentle shove in my back and something was pushed into my hand with a 'This is for you'.

I turned around, swaying port to starboard, but it was too late to identify who had slipped the metallic disc into my palm. I carefully navigated my way through chairs and clusters of inebriated men to a table where I slumped into a vacant seat and began pushing the object around on a film of beer spilt on the tabletop. It was hard at first trying to focus through the smoke, but I determined the thing was the size of a 20-cent piece, with a clip ring slipped through a small hole which had been punched in the disc. It looked like an ID tag, and was slightly bent out of shape. It also had a number and other lettering on it. When I read the inscription I caught my breath. The Phoenician Club faded and then melted away...

SOUTHERN PHUOC TUY, APRIL 1968 – PART 1

My head slammed back against the seat, and the wind-blast through the open port made my eyes gush. It was clear what the smart bastard of an air jockey was trying to do. It was what chopper pilots called 'evade tactics'. Take the stick firmly in both hands and churn it left–right, left–right. Do it hard with plenty of grunt. At the same time do a lawnmower job on the local vegetation by keeping just above tree-top level. The effect on the passenger is the sensation your guts are about to jump out of your mouth; sickening swells wash through the ear canal and you can almost hear your eyeballs click.

Caesar was sitting with his arse on my feet, his two front legs splayed, and his nose pushed up against the perspex bubble, his tongue extended. There was a deliriously euphoric look in his eyes at the trees flashing just yards beneath him. He was ready to orgasm. I was ready to projectile vomit.

'Pays to evade,' the pilot shouted across at me. 'Stops us getting a rocket down the throat,' he grinned, then jabbed a finger at the dog: 'Loves this shit, don't he?'

It hit me for a fleeting moment, what the enemy on the ground would have thought as he peered up at this speeding plastic ball clattering overhead—with a slavering dog gawking down at him. Victor Charlie would have choked on his rice. The pilot pulled the mike over to his mouth and spoke briefly, then slammed the Sioux into a tight 90.

I couldn't hold back throwing up much longer, and squeezed my eyes shut. Maybe blocking out the yawing horizon would keep the hot lava down a little longer. The nausea was triggered by a mixture of air sports and the fear of any moment being blasted out of the sky. Bell Corporation's Sioux H13 was the smallest helicopter in Vietnam, a glass bubble attached to a meccano set tail with two fuel tanks strapped just below the main rotor. A stone from a sling would bring the contraption down. But not with Buck Rogers at the controls. In the bigger Iroquois UH-I you had some semblance of safety. More to the point, you didn't see all the world and your life flashing by through 180 degrees.

'Watch for purple smoke,' the pilot yelled, and began a stomach-heaving climb, squinting through his visor for the smoke grenade which would mark our landing spot.

He swung sharp to port. 'Dead ahead now, there's the New Zealand Company. Get hold of your dog, it'll be hot in and out.' He jerked a thumb upwards: 'By the way, you're gonna get a wet arse.'

I spotted the marker smoke gushing up near a clearing in the jungle at the same time I saw the black storm-front moving in. Afternoon monsoon, you could set your watch by the daily down-pours. Pushing Caesar further into the plastic nose of the Sioux, I untangled my webbing and positioned my rifle barrel down between my feet just as the aircraft's skids thumped down.

The pilot flipped his visor, his face was twisted with the desperation to get up and get out, and he hit my shoulder 'Go! Go…and good luck.'

Dragging my webbing and rifle, and pulling the dog tight to my leg I wobbled across to the tree line and plunged into the security of the gloom. It was as humid as hell. Strapping on basic webbing I tried to shake sweat out of my eyes and adjust to the dark, gradually focusing on three men sitting shoulder-to-shoulder at the base of a tree. They looked like three blokes who had been out on a bushwalk and were taking five for a smoke. I stepped closer and noticed no movement, while Caesar pushed his head forward, cautiously drinking in the scent.

All three Vietnamese had been killed by a burst of automatic fire, their eyes locked open, caught by the violent shock of impact. The sight and the gathering flies didn't help a still upset stomach. I dwelt a moment longer wondering on the perverse minds which had positioned three dead men in such a statement of intimate mateship.

Welcome to the shooting party.

'The boss said he wanted to keep the jungle tidy, so we put 'em 'gainst the tree.' The voice belonged to a monster of a man who seemed to emerge from a cave behind me. He was sipping a hot drink and looking up through the canopy of trees. 'Nice of them to come along, yeh. We were about ready to brew up...and it's gonna fucking rain. Any minute we are in for a wet arse, uh-uh.'

The New Zealand soldier, talking to me and himself, looked part Maori, had the clipped tone of a Kiwi and resembled a huge bullfrog. He had no neck, and an enormous head with a tiny bush hat perched on top. For an absurd moment I thought of Toad in *Wind In The Willows*.

'What do you mean, the boss said he wanted to keep the jungle tidy?' I had never heard the expression. It must have been a New Zealand thing.

'He said he didn't want a lot of rubbish lying about the place. The boss said always leave the jungle as you found it. But these blokes were a bit of a problem.'

'Why not bury them? Only take a minute?'

Mr Toad looked at me like I'd just been beamed in. 'I was making a fucking brew, if you don't mind.'

I noticed the footwear on the dead men were canvas-style boots, no rubber sandals. North Vietnamese Army, NVA? I nudged one of the boots and asked if there were any more. A stupid question; if there were no more I wouldn't be here with the tracking dog.

'More? Any fuckin' more? Jesus, man, where you bin? There's fuckin' hundreds out here. Nogs fuckin' everywhere. But you're gonna find 'em, aren't you boy?' He patted Caesar's head. 'Good looking dog, hey?' He stood up. 'Here's the boss.'

The monsoonal downburst came at the same time the platoon commander slithered up to us...and the same time the first flies fled the corpses. The Kiwi boss leaned forward, hands on knees, and talked to the dog rather than to me. 'I'm putting an M60 behind you. We'll move up the contact position and you can get on it. Could be up to 10 enemy and likely NVA.'

You didn't need a degree to tell the New Zealander was burned out, his face so drawn, pinched, ugly. He was definitely packin' death. Who wouldn't be? It had been hours since the firefight when his scout had bumped the leading enemy trio. The Kiwis had had a fierce exchange, then had tried to follow up the enemy. Being unsuccessful, they had called for a tracking team—a request that had me and three other trackers down to the Nui Dat chopper pad, wheezing and grunting, speculating on where and who had got into the shit this time. Army procedure in an emergency then clicked in: hurry up and wait. And wait.

We waited two hours, I reckoned, for the big Huey to wheel in and do the pick up. It didn't come. Sounding like a sewing machine on full throttle, the little Sioux arrived, a tiny aircraft which had room for one man next to the pilot. He called me over and jerked his thumb toward the single seat next to him: 'You and the dog, that's all, let's go!'

After nearly 12 months of operations, this was becoming the norm; the war was falling to pieces. Things were sloppy, margins for error were narrowing. The tracking team had fragmented from a cohesive unit back in Australia to small units of dog and three men on call-out. Now it was down to just man and dog. The war had changed from hit-and-run actions to big engagements with a different enemy. Local force Viet Cong had become NVA regulars; the tempo had been cranked up; there was a sort of desperation everywhere. The fact that time left in country for 2RAR was short didn't help the nerves. But you didn't try and look at the big picture, if you did you'd go mad. Stick with the Diggers' Vietnam Anthem: Keep your head down, arse up and just keep taking it until RTA (Return to Australia).

Here I now stood in the rain with no qualified visual tracker and no trained coverman to protect me and the dog during the follow-up. The rain was streaming down through the canopy in a thousand small waterfalls. The drumming from above drowned out conversation, and we had to almost yell instructions to each other as we worked our way through the jungle to the contact location. It wasn't hard to find; trees had been shredded by high-velocity bullets and there was bright-red blood leading off down a track.

I strapped Caesar in his harness and took a quick drink of water to wash out the familiar metallic taste that always appeared in my mouth just before a track. But this time the taste, like a mouthful of dirty coins, was accompanied by another feeling. It was a sensation I hadn't really experienced during the tour—I felt absolutely exhausted, fatigued, drained and at the worst mental low I'd been at since arriving in country nearly a year ago.

I was still battling the depression and giving the dog a rub down when three soldiers approached me. One was Mr Toad, now spooning baked beans out of a ration can. They all looked like they had walked out of a black-and-white horror film; that shattered look that stays with men for hours after combat—agitated, twitching with unpredictability, saying very little.

What was there to say? We are about to chase up to 10 wounded, very pissed-off North Vietnamese troops into the jungle, in the rain, hoping they won't see us coming so that we could kill them before they killed us.

The gunner squelched up to me. He had an M60 machine-gun with a 50-round belt hanging off it and another two 100-round belts over his shoulder.

'Boss says you can go when you're ready,' he said. He then came closer to me, eyes averted, looking down the trail. 'You see a single Nog, you fuckin' drop 'cause I'll be over your arse with a full belt going.'

The third man nodded approval. He was the scout, I was sure of that. He was the bloke who zapped the three enemy and would be a definite asset on a mad mission like this. Like me, he nursed an Armalite. And also like me, he was small, ideal for moving quietly through the 'j'. He had a sweat-rag wrapped around his head, but it only served to emphasise two large protruding ears. I guessed in a moment he was called 'Wingnut'.

He watched me shake out the 20-foot tracking lead, and smiled as I spoke quietly to Caesar who was now sporting the drowned-rat look.

'That's a good looking dog, mate,' the scout said. 'You haven't got your usual coverman, nuh? S'okay, I'll be watching for you.'

I should have felt better at the news, but I didn't; tracking in pouring rain was the pits. We could see virtually nothing up ahead through the spray generated by the monsoon and we would have to totally rely on Caesar's point.

I hoisted my rifle and hissed at the dog, 'Seek 'em out. Find 'em boy,' and whispered to myself 'And don't fuck up'. Ahead were only shadows and the vegetation shining and shaking in the downpour. We plunged down the tunnel.

TAKING OVER

It's a straight road. You've got both hands on the wheel. Then you make an irrational decision and take a detour that brings you up outside a weatherboard building with flaking cream paint. The place is the Infantry Training Centre, Ingleburn, New South Wales, and the red-and-white sign on the World War II structure reads TRACKING WING.

It was early 1966. I was 18 years old, had completed basic and infantry training in the past six months, and was now a qualified grunt, 10 foot tall, bullet proof. I also was about to commit one of the Army's cardinal sins: I was about to volunteer for something.

What had brought me to an appointment with one of the training officers was curiosity about the activities only a couple of hundred yards away from the Tracking Wing building. It was there that up to a dozen dogs were undergoing training. I had watched the animals from a distance as they went through obedience training, before they climbed into the back of a big old Studebaker for several days in the bush following human tracks. They were tracking dogs and they were being trained for the war in Vietnam—and I had asked for an interview with a view to getting on board.

One of the motivating factors was that I'd always loved dogs. In my childhood living in Rhodesia (now Zimbabwe), we had always had a dog, from a friendly mongrel to two pedigreed Ridgebacks. My father still had dogs, at last check it was a loopy German-shepherd cross. Could I be an Army dog handler? Warrant Officer Carter, second-in-charge of Tracking Wing, would decide. Another young soldier I had gone through training with was also supposed to be at the meeting, but Blue Murray hadn't yet turned up and I decided to malinger for a minute and lit up a smoke. I had barely taken a drag when Carter suddenly appeared.

Short, stocky, a cap pulled down low over his eyes, he was the typical don't-fuck-with-me Company Sergeant Major, who shit on lower ranks from a great height.

'Private Haran? You're looking at dog handling?'

'Sir,' I spluttered, trying to butt out the smoke.

'Where's your hat?'

'Sir?'

'Where's your hat? What makes you think you can just stroll around here without a bloody hat?'

I was flummoxed. What was this fucking idiot going on about? My hat was on a bench near the door of the hut. I'd taken the thing off…

'Every dog handler must wear his hat,' Carter said, striding on past me up the steps of the hut. 'I've cleared it, you march in tomorrow. See Corporal Eather. And make sure in future you wear your hat.'

The hut door slammed and Carter was gone and I was in the Tracking Wing as a future dog handler. It was as I retrieved my slouch hat that I became aware something or somebody was watching me.

The dog was sitting under a tree near the back of the hut, and the person I assumed was his handler was drinking from a tap. The animal was sitting erect, one ear pointed up, the other flopped to one side, and he was staring straight at me. The stillness in the dog was unnerving, it was almost like he was studying me, measuring me up.

His handler retrieved the lead and spoke to the dog, 'Come on, Caesar.'

As the pair walked away the dog continued to look at me, and I swear he was saying *see you later.*

Next day I lugged my hold-all and webbing down to the Tracking Wing accommodation hut. Carter was standing in front of a blackboard in the Tracking Wing hut. He had just finished sketching a stick man and was now drawing spirals which emanated from the figure. It reminded us of kindy, but this was for grown-up kids and made stuff-all sense to anybody.

'Hair, oil, toothpaste, clothes, breath, boots and dirty socks,' he ticked off with a piece of chalk, drawing more circles around the figure which had scrawled above its head 'ENEMY'.

'Gun oil, wooden stock, even ammunition, it all forms a pattern of smell. A smellscape. It's on the bushes, the leaves, on the ground and hanging in the air.'

In the room there were eight or nine soldiers seated in a semicircle around the blackboard. Six of them were visual trackers, doing the two-week course at the Tracking Wing. Blue Murray and I sat with them, learning the elementaries of scent tracking; what makes a tracking dog track.

Dogs have long noses to house up to 200 million sensory cells which are embedded on 20 square inches of tissue. This is the olfactory centre, which is only about half a square inch in size in humans. When a dog's nose goes down to pick up scent, the moisture around the animal's nostrils dissolves molecules in the air which then settle on the olfactory tissue, a membrane which is a series of folds inside the dog's nose. The odour information is quickly interpreted and sent to the brain.

When a tracking dog is introduced to a scentscape, he will 'lock on' and continue to follow that individual scent signature, even if the quarry attempts to elude him by crossing his smell track with hundreds of other persons.

Carter and his boss, Lieutenant French, had at the beginning of 1966 been charged with forming the Tracking Wing. It was to be modelled on the British Army's tracking teams, which had functioned with success in Malaya and Borneo. The belief was that trackers could also work in Vietnam; it was similar terrain and the war was against guerillas whose techniques were hit and run.

The dog was the 'point' in the team; he did all the work, following the enemy scent at high speed. The visual trackers were responsible for locating the start of the track, assessing enemy numbers and picking up the trail if the dogs lost it. The dog relied on the scent pattern left behind as the guerilla moved through the jungle, and that scent could be just one hour old or have been lingering for days. In the heat and wet of the jungle, the scent would cling to foliage as the quarry moved over the ground. The running man could not help but leave a smell—his breath was enough. Better still if he was dirty and sweating. Better again if he was wounded and leaving a blood trail.

'Scent trails will shift with the wind,' said Carter. 'A dog can be following a scent several yards from the original track the man has made, but he's still on the track and the handler must not try and pull him onto the physical track, even if the visual trackers believe the dog may have lost the trail.'

Carter went on to talk about visual tracking: the leaf overturned by a boot, the broken ants' nest, the damp ground next to the dry ground indicating scuffing by light footwear, and the pattern of vegetation which had turned to show a different colour as a fast-moving party fled through thick bush.

Blue Murray and I had found the transfer to Trackers relatively easy. The requirement was a solid grounding in minor tactics, a desire to work with dogs and an even temperament. We had three weeks to measure up, and to be measured up by Carter and French.

Our first week at Tracking Wing was a non-event—we hadn't been near a dog, and there was a feeling of being lost and adrift in all the activity around us. We were in the hut making our beds when Carter walked by and said, 'You're the enemy for the next two days. Get the VC gear from the store hut.'

Inside an hour we had been briefed by French who gave us a map and compass, 'In case we don't find you,' he said with a smirk. We pulled on dirty shorts and shirts, threw one day's rations into a backpack and drew a rifle and blank ammunition. Our destination was Bulli Pass, thickly forested country near the Pacific Highway, south of Sydney.

The Land Rover driver dropped us off and we set to navigating over a complex route French had marked out. We moved quickly along the cliffs overlooking the east coast and Wollongong before swinging west towards the heavy canopy of forest. It wasn't hard taking bearings; I read a map well and there were huge powerlines up and down that section of the country, ideal reference points. We struggled and grunted over five miles of deadfall, waded through thick waist-high grass, then into clinging lantana, and splashed up a creek before collapsing in a wheezing heap in the forest shade. I checked the compass, took backbearings and told Blue we were about on the cross French had pencilled on the map.

'Let them find us after that and I'll be buggered,' said Blue, already brewing up coffee and having a smoke while we went over the exercise.

The dog team would have left Ingleburn an hour after we had departed. The dog and handler, along with a visual tracking team and Carter, were given a 100-yard wide starting point at the top of the Pass. They had to locate the track, which had been marked with my single large boot scuff somewhere in that 100 yards, then put the dog on the scent. Their mission was to find us without being detected.

Blue and I took turns at sentry from an observation point which gave a good view of the way we had come in. We had a clear field of vision, and were sure we couldn't be sprung by a group of men and a dog coming over open ground. As soon as we saw the trackers we would fire blanks. They would do the same if they surprised us. We talked shit and sipped coffee for half an hour, figuring this was French's way of testing our map-reading–navigation skills. I took first watch while Blue read a *Phantom* comic.

'Do you reckon dogs can detect cigarette smoke over a distance?' I asked, chain-smoking my sixth Marlboro.

Blue was dozing by now. 'Don't be bloody stupid.'

Two hours later I slid down and Blue moved up to the patch of dirt and leaves we had mounded in front of us. I started to urinate when there was a series of deafening rifle shots to my right.

'*Shit, shit…*' Blue rolled over as a visual tracker kicked him behind the shoulder and grinned at me, 'You're pissing down your leg, mate.'

WO Carter stepped into the shadows. 'We were onto you from the other side of the clearing. The dog pointed straight at you.' He turned around, 'Come here, Caesar.'

The handler was unbuckling the harness and had his canteen out to give the dog a drink. I looked at the animal that had just done us cold. He was a labrador–kelpie cross. He was panting, looking at me with one ear up and the other hanging down. He had a solid build, but almost gracefully long legs. I had watched him being put through his paces by his handler during my first days at the kennels, and was told this dog had reached superstar status. In his first months since being bought from an animal welfare home he had broken even the British tracking dog records; he was a freak who could do any distance and track and hold human trails 72 hours old. He virtually never failed to point.

We headed back up to the highway and climbed into a Land Rover for the run back to Ingleburn. I couldn't take my eyes off the dog, who was now snoring on the seat with his head up against his handler's leg. There was an air of the maverick about the animal, a loopiness. If there was a canine equivalent of an Australian larrikin, it was this lop-eared dog. When he lifted his head to look at me, I almost felt he was having a chuckle. '*Gotcha*.'

SOUTHERN PHUOC TUY, APRIL 1968 – PART 2

Behind me Wingnut and Mr Toad were hissing like steam engines, staggering and battling to keep their footing on the narrow track.

Caesar was his nonchalant self, trotting 15 feet ahead of me, occasionally dipping his head for a confirming sniff. The scent, depite the rain, was everywhere: spread though the mud, on the vegetation and hanging in the air. The dog was sucking it up, now locked on to the smellprint I had introduced him to about 20 minutes ago. A sudden gush of enemy odour in the air would trigger a point, an early warning the VC or NVA were no more than 100 yards ahead.

The sensation of tracking through this part of the forest was like drifting through an aquarium. There was almost complete silence now that the rain had stopped, but the air was torpid with moisture and every man was covered in a sheen of sweat.

My mental and physical state had not improved since we started. I still felt fatigued to the point of collapse. I hadn't eaten for two days. That's what a good dose of Nui Dat diarrhoea does for you. Now I was well and truly running on empty. Add to that the anxiety, the loss of concentration, and I was a monty for stumbling head-on into Charlie, tripping a wire, treading on a mine or springing an ambush ...unless Caesar pointed first. I kept willing the dog it was up to him. 'I'm fucked.'

Caesar stopped for his regulation piss and I collapsed down onto one knee, clasping both hands around the barrel of the Armalite as an old man would cling to his crutch. Struggling with my water bottle for a quick drink, I heard Wingnut settle quietly behind me while the machine-gunner leaned against a tree and Mr Toad melted into the shadows.

'Keep goin',' the scout croaked. 'You're doin' well. Any minute I reckon we'll bounce the fuckers.' I felt a gentle tug as Caesar looked back, ready to track on.

Ahead I detected the foliage beginning to break up and splashes of grey sky started to appear. The metallic taste came back to my mouth when I suddenly stepped out onto a wide track cutting across my front. I swore, and pulled Caesar back while I examined the new trail. I cursed again not having a trained visual tracker with me, although Blind Freddie could tell this was a Nogs' main highway.

I called the scout up and showed him the boot tracks and ox cart furrows. 'There's fuckin' dozens of Charlies been using this, and I'm not walkin' straight long into it like taking a Sunday stroll.'

Wingnut looked up and down the main trail and nodded. 'What did the dog say? He reckon there's any Nogs up here?'

'We haven't had a conversation about it, but I'd say there's beaucoup numbers using this as a thoroughfare to market or some fucking thing. We haven't got the firepower to take on these bloody numbers. I hope your boss knows that, mate.'

Wingnut crept back to get the boss while the gunner crouched next to me, his eyes spinning and head rotating like a side show clown with its mouth open.

Mr Toad hunkered down next to me. 'Want to ask you something, matey.' I stared at the big man whose eyes were bulging out at me while at the same time he chomped into a chocolate bar. 'Want to ask you, do you really think there's a Noggie market up here somewhere?'

I wondered if this bloke was retarded.

Wingnut came back. 'Boss said go on and see if the dog points or anything.'

I shot a look of contempt at the scout. 'Or anything? What's "Or anything?"' Wingnut just motioned forward with his weapon.

I stepped out onto the track and whispered to Caesar to seek the enemy. The dog took off at a lope and, now exposed like a wooden figure on a shooting range, I suddenly got my powers of concentration back. The New Zealand rifle platoon stepped out onto the trail one at a time and took up a staggered open-file formation, the correct protocol for walking on tracks and trails—which infantry hated to do in a country where pathways were seeded with mines and booby traps.

The dog was tracking easily, but I felt it was totally unnecessary because this was a main road right into a major enemy position. The taste of metal came into my mouth again—the same time I felt that anal tightening every grunt knows, called packin' death.

Corporal Arthur Eather was a Malayan campaigner who suffered chronic heartburn and dosed daily on milk of magnesia. He explained, with a continuous belch, it was a legacy from years of eating Asian curry, which had led to the inevitable stomach ulcer. He still ate the wrong food, drank and worked and played hard. As chief dog trainer at Tracking Wing, Eather had brought a world of knowledge to the war dog kennels; he knew labradors and what made them tick, and he could pick a winner and a loser. Eather always had his uniform greens starched and pressed with creases so sharp they could cut cheese. He wore the crossed rifles over a green and gold armband that designated him as an instructor.

Four days of the week the dog teams, handlers and staff were out bush and invariably came back covered in layers of filth and greens in tatters. For that reason bush uniform was a scruffy mix of camouflage trousers, British-issue sweat-shirts, US Army boots, and bedding equipment scrounged or bought at Army surplus stores. The trackers did not pull normal duties at the Centre; it was considered their additional duties were looking after more than a dozen dogs that had to be fed, exercised and groomed every day.

WO Carter ignored the bush kit, but insisted on proper dress code at the Infantry Centre. He paid little attention to any form of rigid discipline, accepting the fact that if you made Tracking Wing you knew the drill. Do the right thing, he paid no attention; stuff up and his face contorted from neck to receding hairline and he hissed through his teeth. He was an individual who never stopped moving, a squat, short man who breezed up and down the lines with a clipboard under his arm. He used his words with a clipped economy: 'Peter, new dog in tomorrow. You're taking him over. See Arthur.'

By the time I turned my head he was gone, down the barrack's steps heading to his office.

I stood looking at the dog and realised the Army had dealt me a shitty hand. Damian was a labrador crossed with what we suspect may have been a Rottweiler, but it was hard to tell because of the misshapen head that made the dog the equivalent, in human terms, of a Neanderthal. The back legs splayed out as they met the feet, and the hindquarters seemed higher than the front shoulders, so the dog's back looked like a ski run going the wrong way. Why the heck Carter and French had selected the dog was a mystery. Even to my untrained eye he was ugly. And he was mean-spirited.

I told Arthur Eather I thought my first dog looked and acted like a bloody misfit.

'Bullshit. You can train any dog, anytime,' he said, putting the dogs and handlers through a morning session of obedience training. He watched me and corrected my walk with the dog at the heel; how to use a choker to keep the dog in position; flick the lead in front of his nose to stop him pulling ahead at a slow walk and yank back hard with a single word of command. I was too inexperienced to notice Damian already had my measure and was running a con. I adopted a positive attitude and walked around with plenty of 'Good dog' and 'There's a good boy!'

It took only 15 minutes into his first obedience class for Damian to show his colours. Suddenly I was on my arse looking up at blue sky, the lead burned through my hand and was gone, followed by a roar of protest from other men as Damian grabbed the first opponent around the throat. In seconds we were in the middle of a dog riot, a blur of thrashing, biting, rolling bodies. Eather's shouted instructions to break it up and '*Everyone get your own dog out!*' achieved nothing as the brawl spread from one corner of the paddock to the other.

Men swore among the yelps and howls of pain until eventually each dog was manhandled back to his own corner, straining and foaming with hate to tear apart the vicious newcomer.

'Get him over near the trees and calm him down, *and stay*

there.' Eather ran past me before making a check on the bruised and bleeding victims. Two dogs were carried over to the vet shed for patching and stitching. I was a gasping wreck as I brought a panting and slavering Damian to heel. I wanted to kick the living shit out of the bastard.

Later that afternoon, after feeding time, we took the dogs out for an evening run in the training area near the kennels. I positioned myself a safe distance from the other handlers and let my dog free. Damian looked back at me, shook himself and took off like a missile. In moments he was out of sight. Two hours later he was still out of sight and the sun had gone as I walked around the Inf. Centre with Arthur Eather looking for the latest addition to the war dog kennels. The corporal walked across the training area, muttering, 'Any dog can be trained anytime.'

Later that night I was called up to the guardhouse near the main gate. The guard sergeant came to the door, yelling, 'There's a labrador running loose over at the married quarters, and the adjutant's not too happy about some mongrel screwing his pedigree Afghan. They reckon it's one of our bloody tracking dogs.'

With the night duty corporal trying to keep a straight face, I collected Damian from a stone-faced captain and threw him into the back of the Land Rover. Next morning Arthur Eather took me aside for a short talk, and we went through some basic obedience with the incorrigible canine who, on his third day, was shaping up as the Loser of the Year.

Damian was unmanageable. Was it me? I drank all weekend, nursing a growing depression. Other handlers came by with advice, or a quip about fuckwit dogs matching their shitwit handlers.

Lying on the cot I reassured myself: even if I did have a psycho dog, how come some of the best dogs in the kennels had some of the dumbest handlers? Good blokes they were, but occasionally you had to question their IQ.

Take Tex from Armidale in the New England Range. The way Tex told it, it was horses, cattle and cowboy country. I didn't know what they did in Armidale, but Tex certainly was a bushman—from the boots and weathered jeans he always wore into town down to the drawl and nasal twang. He was a good six foot and when he put his dog through obedience he looked like Cheyenne Bodie with a dachshund. He was laidback, easy-going and full of bush philosophy—a mood that would switch to a foul and destructive temper after a few beers.

Fergie was the trained dog handler to tracking dog Marcus. Fergie came from Redcliffe in Queensland, was about half the height of Tex and would also undergo a mood change after several jugs of beer. The fact Tex would take on all comers during a drunken rage didn't worry Fergie, who would call his taller opponent out for a fistfight without hesitation. The two going at it outside the hut would qualify for the main attraction in a circus freak show.

Then there was Polly who hung out with Tex. Polly was an ex-clerk from Melbourne who joined the Army for overseas service. Problem was, Polly had a bad acne condition and the medicos at Ingleburn couldn't fix it up. Polly stood for hours under the shower pouring white goo all over himself and soaping it in. But the prescription guk did nothing for the acne, and Polly returned from the shower block a pale prune depressed he would not get to Vietnam.

'Sweat and acne will keep me out of 'Nam,' Polly said. 'I've gotta get rid of one or the other.'

Tex's compassionate nature came to the fore and he declared to us all he would get rid of Polly's skin complaint. He punched his mate on the shoulder and said: 'Tomorrow night we go down to the Rails and get pissed. We come back and I give you a shave.'

Polly looked at Tex with a stupefied expression on his face. The rest of us wondered what the punchline would be to a lengthy booze session at the Railway Hotel in Liverpool then a visit to the showers. Tex just winked and said not to worry, he'd seen the special acne treatment work before in the Armidale high country.

Next morning in the Tracking Wing hut the shit was hitting the fan. The guard sergeant was standing over Polly's bed, and the word was out for Carter and French to report early for an inquiry into a 'serious incident'. Tex was nowhere in sight.

Polly refused to get out of bed and was whimpering to the duty sergeant. 'He said stand still and he'd scrape it all off.' Polly eventually sat up and allowed the blanket to fall from his face, which was a mass of nicks, cuts and lacerations up to an inch long. The dog handler looked as if he'd walked into a high-speed fan. The duty sergeant had tracked Polly down after being told a screaming soldier was bleeding to death in the shower block and was being forcibly shaved by a drunken or deranged digger. There were now serious threats of a charge for self-inflicted injury. Polly refused to name his attacker and pulled three weeks' kitchen duties for the failed miracle acne treatment.

Polly and Tex waged war for weeks after the shaving episode, with Tex maintaining acne could be scraped off the face or any other part of the body with a sharp cut-throat razor. The fact that Polly went along with the outrageous stunt prompted Fergie to suggest Polly 'get a fucking psych report done, never mind about the fucking acne.'

Polly burned for revenge against his big drinking mate and retaliated by force-feeding a full bottle of beer to Tex's dog before a practice bush track. The result was Tex lost for hours in the Bulli forest.

On the Monday Eather came to me with reassurance about Damian. 'We'll take him out to Bulli with the other dogs today and see if a change of scenery does any good.'

About a dozen handlers loaded their dogs into the big old Studebaker and I climbed up last, seated myself next to the tailgate and pushed Damian almost completely under the bench seat. Other handlers held their animals in a sitting or lying position between their legs for the long drive south.

Eather pushed the truck at full throttle, grinding through the gears as we swung off the highway onto the trail along the cliff where Blue and I had laid a track weeks earlier. Heavy rain began falling across the escarpment. The dogs had all gone into a doze and I was nodding off as we rocked and rattled further into the training area.

What shook me awake was the roar of the spinning tandem wheels in the mud on the cliff track. Soldiers suddenly dropped comics and books and pulled their dogs more tightly in between their legs. The truck was digging further into the mud as Eather crashed through the gears. We were sliding back, and could now clearly see the cliff below, hundreds of yards downwards a tangle of trees and rock face overlooking the coast. At that moment Damian started his second bout with 11 other dogs.

The screams of pain and the shouts alerted Eather something was seriously wrong in the back of the

Studebaker. I swore at myself for not noticing my bloody dog had crawled along, beneath the bench seat, until he selected his moment to launch an attack. The roll and slide had taken the heavy truck to within two yards of the cliff edge. Eather had yanked on the handbrake before jumping down into the rain.

'*Get out. Just get out now!*' He was pulling back the front part of the tarpaulin so men and dogs could escape from the front of the vehicle. Handlers and dogs spewed from the Studebaker, tumbling, sliding and stumbling, then collapsing in the mud. I threw Damian, with his fangs still buried in another dog, out of the truck and jumped clear. There was a sudden silence after the screaming, and I felt a dozen pair of eyes lock on me. Arthur Eather clutched his stomach as his ulcer erupted and threatened to charge the next man who said he was going to throw Damian over the cliff.

It was later that week the chief dog instructor took a swig of milk of magnesia, drew a 9mm from the armory and made his way down to the kennel marked 'Damian.' I watched as he slid a packet of biscuits into his pocket then slipped the choker chain over the dog's neck. He closed the kennel door and walked past me. 'Grab a shovel. There are some dogs you can't train anytime.'

I trailed behind the pair, out to the training area and watched as Eather threw a biscuit onto the ground. The dog bent to pick it up and I heard the Browning being cocked. There was a sharp crack as a single round entered a point just behind Damian's ear. I buried the dog and then walked back through the trees alone.

A deep feeling of frustration and failure came over me that week. I had become the pariah of the Tracking Wing, the one 'who had that bloody mad dog'. Damian had been a renegade, an animal with a flaw that couldn't get past first base in the Army. Trying to bite Eather when we got back from the Bulli debacle was the last straw, I figured. The bullet had been the best and safest way out because we couldn't give the dog away to a civilian.

I accepted the facts of the situation and spent the next few days with Blue Murray laying tracks for Cassius and Justin, who were in final preparations for posting to the 7th Battalion at Puckapunyal. Caesar and Marcus were also close to completing training before transfer to the 2nd Battalion in Brisbane. They would be the first Australian tracking dogs to join tracking teams and do a year's duty in Vietnam. It was during a severe attack of the blues I was called in to see French and Carter.

The two men were standing chatting, looking out of the Tracking Wing office windows at the kennels when I entered. French was the first to speak. 'There's a problem with Caesar. His handler's going to Reinforcement Wing.'

I waited with a dumb look on my face. What was all this to do with me?

Carter, in his usual whirlwind manner, spoke next. 'We want you to take over the dog and get ready to march out to 2RAR. See Arthur. We've had a talk about intense training, because you've got a lot of ground to make up after the problems with that other dog.'

Carter never mentioned by name any dog who failed. A moment later he was gone. I walked from the office barely able to breathe, much less speak. In less than two minutes I had gone from the bottom of the pile to the top of the heap.

WAR DOG D6N03

I bolted breakfast and made my way down to the war dog kennels. Day one with the Top Dog. How would I shape up, shell-shocked after the Damian experience?

The kennels resembled a long set of horse stables. The front block housed 12 dogs in large, airy kennels, basically besser block with concrete floors that extended from the kennel through to an outdoor run of arcmesh where the animals could all see each other. Each dog had one handler in what was a strictly one-on-one relationship; the soldier was responsible for every facet of the dog's life and wellbeing.

Morning routine started with a run across the training area, then back to the kennels for a half-hour grooming. Dog and handler then went through 30 minutes of obedience. This was followed by a thorough clean out of the kennels, scrubbing them down with disinfectant. At least once a week while in camp the dogs were taken on a walk around Ingleburn township where they were made to trot on the road to harden their feet. It was also a chance to familiarise them with traffic. Once a month there was a day at the rifle range during live firing. Here the animals were studied for their reaction to gunfire, a vital test for any war dog, and a skittish animal could be dropped from the training course.

All the dogs were in various stages of training; from the novice doing five-minute-old tracks, to the fully-trained animals who were following up to 10 miles of trail more than a day old. Caesar was working at his peak, and this was where I was at an acute disadvantage. All handlers had gone through complete training, taking their dogs from day one to their current level. I was coming in totally inexperienced, with no idea how to carry out any form of dog handling, from basic obedience to doing a track. It was with this foremost in my mind that I met Arthur Eather at the kennels.

The corporal sat on a dog-biscuit container outside the infirmary, a two-room block where they carried out first aid, prepared worm treatments and stitched up dog-fight victims. Eather was suffering the effects of a night out and rubbing his stomach, grimacing at the pain from the ulcer. I had meant to speak with him about getting the damned thing seen to, but I'd heard he was trying to keep it quiet to get his 20 years up and get his pension.

'First up, we'll spend two days getting you bonded with him, a long walk, lots of play and some light obedience. By day three we'll see how you go over the obstacle course. Then more obedience and then next week, maybe, a track. We've got stuff-all time to do all this, but not to worry, we'll get there, and I'll walk you through each step.'

Eather went to the storeroom and came back with an equipment issue. I walked over to Caesar's kennel with a tracking and walking lead, choker chain and nylon tracking harness. The dog's brush and comb were already next to the grooming pole, which was in the lawn area out front of the kennel block. The dogs were tied to these grooming poles when the kennels were being hosed out. Caesar already had his collar on. A dog tag was attached to it and read D6N03, indicating he was the third dog taken into the kennels in 1966 and his state of origin was New South Wales.

I walked to the run at the rear of the kennel and Caesar came out and jumped up on the arcmesh fence, then flopped on his backside and we had a good look at each other.

He lacked the bulk and wobble of the traditional labrador. This dog had the strong wiry characteristics of the kelpie.

He stood high on long lean legs and boasted a sleek, black medium-length coat and a bushy tail that was usually erect. But it was his face that demanded attention: a long nose, flat forehead and deep-set eyes that burned with intelligence. The dog looked you straight in the eyes. That was disconcerting at first, as most dogs took eye contact with humans as a challenge. Then there was the Caesar trademark: his left ear, with a piece missing, flopped to one side when he tried to hold them both up. The dog was built for the long run, he was an Australian working dog who could take the knocks and keep going without fear of burnout. Some said he was inexhaustible. Rounding off the champ was the fact he was gifted with a phenomenal sense of smell.

We watched each other, and I spoke his name. He came back over to the fence and playfully bit my hand as I shoved it through for a lick.

SOUTHERN PHUOC TUY, APRIL 1968 – PART 3

I took another break and stepped off the trail. Fuck it, I had made my mind up, I was not going to get my arse shot off on this track. The platoon behind me came to a halt and we all strained to hear anything that would indicate an enemy presence. I reined Caesar in and tried to get a drink into him. Mr Toad crept up behind me and knelt while I took a swig myself. 'Eh, digger.' Toad nudged me while forcing two biscuits and a lump of cheese into his mouth.

This guy was giving me the shits. He stayed so close I kept worrying he would walk straight into me and then straight over me. And, hell, he made a huge target for an RPG—a rocket propelled grenade.

'Want to ask you somethin.' Why is your dog black?'

I looked around at the man, thinking I had misheard him. No, his intent look told me he was serious.

'Well, he's black lab cross…a cross kelpie…'

'Yeh, but why do you have a black one instead of a brown one or somethin'?'

'He's just a fucking black dog, right!' Wingnut shot me a look to quieten down. I strained again to hear any sounds coming down the track, chopping, talking…I felt another nudge from Mr Toad.

'What fucking now?'

'I wanted to ask you, mate, does your dog get cross a lot?'

I spat in disgust and shook out the lead. Tracking into a swarm of NVA armed to the teeth with rocket launchers was preferable to dealing with this cretin. But then I felt, oh shit, he was a well-meaning retarded fuck who just asked questions all the time. Like the dog handler I remembered from Ingleburn Tracking Wing who'd always answer a question with 'Why do you ask?' Every bloody minute of the day it was 'Why do you ask?'

'Hey, you reckon it's going to rain today?' The prick would answer 'Why do you ask?'

One day Blue Murray got so pissed off he said to me, 'I've bloody had him. Why do you ask this, why do you ask that.' Blue confronted Why Do You Ask and asked, 'Hey, fucknuckle, can I screw your sister?'

The soldier looked up with why do you ask? all over his face, then turned red with anger. 'You trying to be a smart arse, Blue?'

Quick as a flash Blue shot back, 'Why do you ask?'

I heard a scrunch behind me and turned to see Mr Toad unwrapping a chocolate bar. He was fully switched on covering his arcs, but, God, he was stuffing his face again. I couldn't help it and snarled 'Do you ever stop eating?'

The huge man looked at me almost childlike and shook his head. 'No, why do you ask?'

Before I could scream and bring an enemy battalion down on our heads, Wingnut clicked his tongue to get my attention. He jabbed his finger down the track. 'I can smell fuckin' Noggies, mate…'

Partnering Up

'Turn and watch the dog! Don't let him go on. *Move faster!*'
I turned upsidedown inside the galvanised iron drainpipe, my webbing almost wedging me solid while I groaned and heaved forward. The tunnel water–obstacle was the most difficult in the course. You got down on hands and knees and crawled through, immediately exiting onto a 10-foot long slippery log over a water trench. As soon as you pulled yourself out of the tunnel it was a balancing act on the log, then four quick paces across the water without falling into the stinking brown pool below.

Arthur Eather watched the sideshow. 'Now let the dog loose, he'll go over. *Let him go!*'

Caesar had reached the end of the tunnel, seen daylight and pulled to go across the log. I got out and stood up, still holding the leash, and the dog jumped forward. There was never any doubt where I was going. With one leg forward and the other stuck out sideways, I stumbled forward: knee hit wood, jab of pain, then a sideways roll into the water.

Gasping from the cold dunking, I spewed water and grappled for a hold on the muddy bank. Caesar sat looking down, head turned with a look of amusement.

'I said to let him go when you got out. Do it again.' Eather turned away and I flopped up beside the animal.

During obedience sessions the instructor watched and gently guided me while I stood in front of the dog. Words of command, Eather explained, always went with hand signals. 'It's much like field signals in the section drills,' he said, putting his arm next to his leg for *heel* and *come*, closed fist against his chest for *sit*, outstretched palm for *stay*, and a downsweep of the arm for Caesar to *go down*.

Caesar already knew the drill, but he knew I didn't. He sniffed at the ground instead of watching me, and stared skywards for a bird when I called and motioned him.

'Take control, Peter, take control and show him you are in control. The dog knows, he senses your authority. Go and talk to him.'

I walked over to where the dog was sitting, licking himself. I grabbed him by the collar. 'Caesar sit,' hand against chest. 'Caesar down!' finger pointing to the ground. There was a momentary look of challenge then he sat. 'Better.'

Eather walked over. 'Not "better," wrong word. Listen, when the dog carries out the command it's "Good dog". When he doesn't, it's "No". And repeat it again and again. Drum it in. Your voice must have confidence and authority every time, and there's never any need to shout, never a need to be brutal. Try it again.'

We gave the dog another 20 minutes, took a break and did another 10, and I was improving because Caesar was paying attention. Eather lit up a smoke and sat on a biscuit tin while we sipped morning tea. In the distance other handlers were still at obedience session. The instructor belched with pain then started speaking.

'There is no question obedience will be one of the most important parts of dog handling in Vietnam. This dog must do everything by signal, and I mean everything. Every word of command will be used. I did it all in Malaya, never thought obedience was important, but it is, and at some stage you will need it. It could be a life-saver. It's as important that the dog carries out your every command as it is that you carry out the command of your platoon commander. He's an army dog and he's got to follow orders, your orders. Don't let the little fucker con you.'

The third week of my partnering-up process we went bush, down to the thick, wet forest at Bulli Pass. I travelled with Eather in the Land Rover, while two visual tracking instructors and Blue drove ahead. I wore a belt and water bottle, long-sleeved shirt and bush hat. We all brewed up before the track. Moose, a mountain of a man standing an easy six foot eight inches and weighing in at 18 stone, was the Tracking Wing's chief visual tracker. He would lay obvious signs on the mile-long track, Blue would go with him to strengthen the scent, while Arthur Eather and the second visual tracker travelled with me. It was unlikely to happen, but the visual tracker would recover the trail if the dog lost it.

'Caesar's done this dozens of times,' Eather said while we waited an hour for Moose and Blue to lay the track. 'To him it'll be shit easy. You're going to find it hard. Keep the pace down to start with, and keep talking to the dog. Don't fall and break your friggin' neck.'

The two men watched me buckle on the harness and shake out the tracking lead. We quickly located the boot scuff-mark which started the trail. I put the dog near the mark and said 'Seek!'

Caesar took off quietly, nose down and progressed 50 feet before going into a hunch and defecating. Eather and the visual tracker chuckled at my look of anti-climax. 'S'okay. He's gotta go, he's gotta go.'

Without a word from me the dog took off again. It was a fast walk, and so casual I often thought we must be off the track. But whenever I was about to pull up and question what was happening, I'd spot a boot print or bush deliberately broken by Moose and Blue.

There was little strain on the lead as I extended it over the open ground and shortened it up when we entered thick undergrowth. Moving through the forest was almost completely silent, apart from my heavy breathing. Caesar frequently put his head up or drifted off the trail, cast himself in a circle and resumed tracking.

'Look! *Look!* Watch him now!' Eather's urgent shout behind me brought me back to watching the dog just as he lifted his ears erect. 'That's a point, Peter. They're up front.'

I pulled Caesar up and he immediately lay down, panting. He looked over his shoulder at me like I was stupid. I got the message. As far as he was concerned his job was completed. Blue and Moose emerged from the high ground, yawning. I couldn't believe we'd done a mile.

'Harness off straight away, give him a small drink,' said the instructor, walking over to Moose who shook his head with a knowing grin after a few short words. He and Blue then turned and disappeared into the forest while we sat down to make coffee. Eather squatted, sipping his brew and spoke: 'This time we'll give it another hour and another mile. Moose will throw some funnies in and won't mark the trail so clearly. I want you to pick up the pace…and watch for that bloody point.'

By dusk I was a bloodied mess. My clothes were torn and I'd taken several bad falls. Moose and Blue had laid a trail of S-bends and backtracks—where they'd walked backwards for several yards then swung off in a new direction, left or right—and continually twisted from high ground to low thickets. Caesar had stuck to the track like a magnet, while Eather urged me to walk faster and watch the dog's head. I had tripped, fallen, stumbled and been dragged uphill and down rocky outcrops.

Above: Sketch of Caesar by official Vietnam War artist Ken McFayden, 1968. McFayden spent 12 months with the 2nd Battalion and created this, the only official sketch of an Australian tracker dog from the Vietnam War. (Australian War Memorial/ART 40657)

Above: Ready for Combat. The author and Caesar shortly after arrival at a fire support base, January 1968. Steel helmets and flak jackets were worn instead of the usual jungle wear of shirt and floppy bush hat during road convoys and village searches, to protect against possible mine explosions.

Top: Dogs of War. The Tracking Wing at the Infantry Centre, Sydney, 1967. The author and Caesar are far right; Norm and Cassius, the dog that died in Vietnam, are third from right; Fergie and Marcus are fourth from right. In the centre with peaked caps are instructors Warrant Officer Carter (left) and Lt. French.
Bottom: The Tracking Team in Action. From left, Fergie and war dog Marcus; Les, the coverman; Thatch, the machine-gunner; the author and Caesar. (*The Anzac Battalion in South Vietnam, 1967-68* by K.E. Newman)

Top: Home. Tracking Team and Anti-Tank Platoon tents at Nui Dat. Notice the height of the rubber trees, which often collapsed across the tents; and the sandbagged blast walls to protect against mortar or rocket fire.
Bottom: A Dog's Home. Tracking Team kennels at Nui Dat.

Top: On Parade. The author with Caesar and platoon commander Lt. Leo Van de Kamp at Nui Dat for the 2nd Battalion's birthday.

Bottom: Dog Day Afternoon. Marcus taking some 'R and R' in a hammock with an Anti-Tank soldier during a break at Nui Dat.

Top: Ops Briefing. Tracking Team and Anti-Tank Platoon are briefed before an operation. Bob points to the map board; Thatch and Blue are to his left.
Bottom: The Workhorses of the War. Australian choppers awaiting refuelling at Luscombe Field, Nui Dat. (R. Moodie)

Top: A Light Moment. Julian, one of the longest serving tracker dogs in Vietnam. He served with 3RAR, was posted to 9RAR, and was serving with 8RAR with handler Len Taylor (left) and coverman Rusty Morley in January 1970. (Australian War Memorial/WAR/70/29/VN)

Bottom: 'In the J'. Tracking Team and Anti-Tank members search a Viet Cong base camp.

Top: Man and Dog. Fergie cools Marcus in a stream during operations. (R. Moodie)

Bottom: Trackers. The 2nd Battalion Tracking Team. The author is second from left with Caesar; Fergie is at front with Marcus; Thatch, with machine-gun, crouches beside Fergie; fourth from left is Corporal Bob; second from right is Corporal Bill; and the 'twins' Simon (far left), and Ken (far right). (R. Moodie)

I cursed and winced when I dropped the tracking lead and raced to catch it again while the dog moved forwards, ignoring me. Moose ended the trail with a backtrack at the bank of a creek. The three-foot drop to the water was concealed by heavy ferns, and as Caesar detected the deception he swung and jumped around to recover the scent. I blundered on, by this time not caring where the dog was taking me, whether he had the track, and even if he would point. The tracking trace wrapped around my knees and my final recollection was of somersaulting into the stream and sinking into the mud.

On the bank Eather was waiting, holding Caesar by the harness. The visual tracker was lighting up a smoke, his hands and shoulders shaking so much from coughing and laughing he couldn't keep the match still. Moose and Blue were on their way over.

Eather wasn't happy with the big man, who simply grunted with a grin. 'You said throw in a few wobblies and I did it. And what's the matter with a cool splash before you go to bed?'

'He's just learning mate, give him a go,' said Eather, pulling me up. 'That was a backtrack. Watch the dog as he moves around and casts, and don't just plough blindly ahead. Stand still, watch. Move again as soon as the dog moves off. Next time that could be a punji pit or a mine, not a creek bank.'

Moose bent down and rubbed my head. 'That was a tough one for you first time out, Pete. But the dog held it all the way through. Wait until we get up to 10 miles at Helensburgh.'

Pissed off as I was, Moose wasn't the sort of bloke you picked a serious argument with. I just said, 'Helens who?'

Warrant Officer Carter stood looking out across the military training area commonly referred to as Helensburgh. It was a cool morning, the sun hadn't long been up, but the forecast was for a scorcher. Moose sat on the ground next to the Land Rover eating three hamburgers he'd bought on the drive down from Ingleburn. I hadn't figured how he'd found a burger shop open on the way down, but I was sure he'd have to get them down quick. Next to him, all eyes on the dripping burger meat, was Marcus, a slobbering pedigreed labrador, oblivious to his handler, Fergie, who was checking his pack before the exercise started.

I was doing the same. We had full battle-kit for the 10-mile track: a set of webbing with belt and shoulder harness and main pack. On the waist-belt were two basic pouches with Owen submachine-gun magazines, a machete, two water bottles and a bumpack at the rear which held a groundsheet and bedroll. In addition, the backpack held rations for two days, two cans of dog food, and Fergie and I had shoved another water bottle inside. On the outside of the pack was a short entrenching tool, or shovel. This was battle dress, presumably what we'd wear in Real Combat. In fact it was old-fashioned, out-dated rubbish from World War II.

Helensburgh was undulating country between Appin and Highway One on the east coast, south of Sydney. It was low bush, stunted gum trees and waist-high black boys. There were rocky outcrops and ravines, and the soil was sandy. Here and there in the singularly unspectacular country were giant anthills. It was the sort of scenery that never attracted a second look from those motoring down the coast road.

What made the landscape even more unattractive was its frequency of bushfires. The result was that most of the low bush was blackened and much of the ground was fine ash that rose in clouds as you travelled through, which clogged your nostrils and made the eyes sting.

Carter wore just a belt and water bottle, and carried his customary long wooden staff, his snake-killer stick, as he called it. I noticed a smoke grenade attached to his belt. He was waiting impatiently for Moose to finish his hamburgers before instructing him on the track laying. It was a formality, because both men knew the terrain well from days conducting visual tracking courses in the Helensburgh area. Two other visual trackers were out for the day, dozing in the Land Rover waiting for the word to go. Arthur Eather was not here for the assessment trail. Carter would run the test that would see both dogs qualify for posting to 2RAR.

There was still a great deal of tracking work ahead, much of it at Helensburgh, but the 10-mile track was a pass mark that had to be obtained according to Tracking Wing protocol; it was serious business for handler and dog. Fail, and it was back to five-milers.

Moose was up and pulling a map out of his shirt. He carried an SLR standard infantry rifle and had shoved a handful of blanks into his pocket, grinning at dogs and handlers as he strode past. *What was the cunning bastard going to do this time?* The man was so big the SLR looked like a toothpick in his huge hands. He conferred with Carter for a minute then walked over to the vehicle and tapped on the window. 'Let's go.'

The last I saw of Moose was his head bobbing above the other two trackers in the distance.

Carter walked to the back of the Land Rover and pulled out two Owen machine carbines. They were fitted with canvas slings from butt to barrel. Fergie and I could support the weapons over our shoulders to carry them at a ready position, while our other hand was free to control the tracking lead. The OMC was a legendary weapon; it had been standard issue on Kokoda. It was now obsolete, like the load we were packing. In Vietnam we would carry Armalites, Colt AR-15s or M16s.

'Marcus goes up first,' said Carter. 'We'll break at five miles and then Caesar takes up the track. This is a distance and time trial, but don't rush, or we'll lose it, and watch for snakes. Go in 30.'

Carter went back to the Land Rover.

'*Don't rush it!* We'll hardly be breaking land-speed records with all this crap.' Fergie tried to swing the pack up on his back, missed and tried again. When he had it on with all the other equipment he almost disappeared. I was a slight five foot nine, but Fergie made the Army with barely an inch to spare on the minimum height requirement, and now he wobbled under his load.

Marcus was slurping up the last of Moose's onions from the ground when we made our way to the start of the track. Carter watched Fergie hook up Marcus, adjust his OMC and hiss, 'Seek 'em boy!'

Caesar trotted when he tracked. Marcus used the ram-and-smash approach, virtually flattening the vegetation as he thundered through the scrub, nose down, snorting and wheezing, his tail spinning like a propeller. Fergie was pulled along like a skier at the end of his lead, but after more than a year tracking, dog and handler worked in unison. Fergie dropped the lead and retrieved it as he detoured around thick clumps of bush. He expertly lifted the lead when Marcus went into a casting circle and, despite the labrador's speed, kept the pace down to a fast walk.

Two miles out I was sweating and my throat was on fire after travelling straight through a heavily burnt-out area. Caesar trotted alongside me, seemingly unconcerned, tongue lolling out. By four miles we were all covered in scratches and blackened from encounters with fire-ravaged trees and bushes. Helensburgh was the sort of country you never would have thought would try you, no mountains or jungle humidity. But in the middle of summer it physically and mentally drained you, and your concentration evaporated.

After five miles Marcus was snorting like a steam train and showing signs of fatigue. He hit the ground with a thud when we stopped for an extended break. Fergie fell alongside him and threw off his pack with a grunt.

'Dog's not fit, Fergie. I want a weight check done and a few more five-mile runs.' Carter squatted, taking a long slug from his canteen. I noticed, despite his weight, the WO was showing no sign of exertion while I was panting with exhaustion, then realised I still had 50 pounds on my back. We sat in silence for 15 minutes, then I buckled up Caesar.

After just a short distance I discovered I had got to the bad leg of the 10-miler. The ground dropped, and I struggled to keep the dog back as we descended into a sharp ravine. The load on my back was sapping my energy and the backpack straps were biting into my shoulders. Adding to the frustration was the Owen, which snagged every tree I came near; I fought to keep my cool every time I tripped and fell. Watching the dog for a point only added to the tension of the track, and knowing Carter was watching didn't help. The Helensburgh 10-miler tested dog and handler. Could and would the dog hold the scent through difficult ground? And could the handler stay alert while the heat and hardship intensified? I felt my focus shifting from the dog to the country around me, and had to struggle to get my eyes back on Caesar's head and ears.

Eight miles and he was travelling with his usual lupine lope: sniff here and there, trot on; sniff left, sniff right. A quick relieving wee on a convenient bush. You would swear he was walking around the block on a sunny Sunday. My mind swung back to Moose and the 'enemy' and how far they were now ahead. Would he hit from the high ground? Ambush left or right? I was becoming more distressed from the heat and the weight on my back when suddenly the dog's head shot up and his ears stood out like TV antennae.

I dropped to my knees and pulled up my weapon. Carter stopped and quietly knelt behind me. Ahead the ground rose to a solid group of bushes, an obvious spot for Moose and co. But Caesar had definitely pointed to the right front— waist high grass, flat ground. Carter was watching me to see how I called it; how I read the point.

I turned and indicated the low grass and whispered with thumb down 'enemy'. Carter eased the smoke canister from his belt, pulled the pin and flipped the clip before throwing it in a long arc into the grassed area. There was a pop and a whoosh of purple smoke followed by yells.

Carter stood up and called out 'Come on, Moose, hamburger time'.

The Warrant Officer walked back and rubbed Caesar's head, 'Well done, champ. Good one, Peter.'

He patted Marcus's head on the way back. 'How do you think you'll go in Vietnam, Fergie? I think you'll do okay. You're too short to be shot.'

We did several more tracks at Helensburgh, and both dogs increased time and distance. With each track I grew more confident handling the dog. I learned all the tricks with the 20-foot trace line and how to regulate the pace. I also found I could now read Caesar as he worked; he hopped and jumped around at times like a kangaroo. It was a most unusual tracking method where he alternated between casual stroll to frantic search if he lost the scent. His point was unmistakable, I could pick up on it every time.

SOUTHERN PHUOC TUY, APRIL 1968 – PART 4

It was a classic point. Caesar's ears shot out, he went rigid and his whole body froze. It was so sudden I nearly had an infarction, and dropped to one knee, bringing the Armalite up to my shoulder. I carefully examined the ground ahead—nothing but almost impenetrable stands of bamboo. Looking at Caesar again I figured something was not quite right with that point. It was more like he was having a stand-off during a friendly fight with Marcus than indicating enemy ahead. I gave the inverted thumb sign for enemy to the soldiers behind me and heard them hit the ground taking up firing positions.

'What's going on?' Wingnut had his rifle forward, ready to pull back into his shoulder, and was staring at me. Mr Toad looked like he had swallowed a tennis ball, his bulbous eyes protruding from his head.

I spoke to the two men and the gunner who was stock still on the ground with his finger inside the M60 trigger guard and already squinting along the sights: 'There's more bloody traffic along here than in Martin Place, and I reckon the enemy's in that lot.' I jerked a thumb at the bamboo, which was now rustling, with small sounds carrying out to us like men preparing to open fire.

Before I could wind Caesar in Mr Toad hissed to me 'Eh, digger?'

'What?'

'Want to ask you something.'

'For God's sake, what?'

'Where's that Martin Place place?'

'Chrissake...'

Suddenly the bamboo exploded into life and the gunner pulled his M60 into his shoulder. 'Here they fuckin' come! Contact front!' He squeezed the trigger and held it down, the machine-gun chewing through 50 rounds in less than six seconds.

CELEBRITY DOG

Two Hueys sat on the football oval near the kennels. I'd heard them come in earlier in the morning. We assembled with four dogs near the Iroquois choppers sitting silently with their rotors tied down.

'Approach the aircraft from 10 and two o'clock so the pilot can see you,' said the flight instructor, dressed in a light-green flying suit, General MacArthur sunnies and helmet tucked under his arm.

'We'll give you thumbs up when we see you. Keep your heads down and enter through the starboard and port doors. Buckle in, and the doors will be closed by the crew.'

WO Carter was watching from the trees, and he moved back when the chopper started up. We were using only one of the aircraft. I wasn't sure why the other one was there but apparently the RAAF operated on the 'nun principle', where they went everywhere in pairs. We were lined out at 10 and two o'clock, and Caesar was sitting alongside me. Marcus and Fergie were to my front, and across the other side Cassius and Justin were in position with their two handlers. Caesar was watching the whipping blade, which was slicing through the air with a whoosh and a thwack. Then he went beserk.

For a second I was thrown off balance as he tried to tear away towards the shuddering chopper. '*Shit!* Bloody hell!' The lead burned through my hand as the dog went into a high leap for the blades like a football player going for a high mark.

Carter was suddenly alongside me. '*Grab and hold him.* What the hell's going on?'

I mumbled 'dunno' just as the pilot gave a thumbs up

through the cockpit window to get on board. Marcus and Fergie ran forward, and Cassius and Justin were on their way. I went for broke, grabbed Caesar by the collar and wrenched him forward. He was half way up my body, his nails scraping at my flesh, when I reached the aircraft door and flung him inside. The pilot turned with an amused grin as the door slammed shut and we were moving forward and up.

I grunted relief. What the heck was that all about? I grabbed Caesar's nose and mouth and pulled him towards me. 'Try that stunt again and I'll fuckin' bop you one!'

He slumped to the floor and settled with the other three dogs for the short joy-ride around Ingleburn. Fergie looked across at me and shrugged with a grin, 'Stuffed if I know.'

It was the same hellish behaviour on landing when we scrambled off the machine, with me pulling the dog down out of the air where he was spinning like a wind chime. Even at a distance from the helicopter he was foaming, and I physically twisted him down to the ground.

I sat quietly during the tea break, dumbstruck by his reaction to the choppers. I had every reason to worry about the situation, considering the tracking dog would spend half his life in choppers when we started operations in Vietnam.

Later that day, it was time for winch drill; another first for the dogs. The winch jacket was basically a rectangular piece of canvas with three buckles and a D-ring on top. It enclosed the dog so just their head, legs and rear-end hung loose. We had already tried the device on a rope over a tree bough, and the only reaction had been a woe-is-me look on the face of a labrador swinging loose 20 feet off the ground.

Another mad minute as I got Caesar on board and the pilot took the machine straight up to 50 feet, where I strapped on the winch harness. We went higher, and the crewman clipped the winch hook on the D-ring and swung the dog out into space. Before Caesar had time to figure where he was, the winch button was depressed and he went into gentle free fall towards terra firma and two handlers waiting below. Marcus then went out the door with a sook-look on his face.

Excercise over, we walked back to the kennels, where I sought out Arthur Eather who was having a quiet smoke in the vet room.

'So, talk to me, how'd it all go?' the corporal said.

'I think I've found the dog's weak point. He can track well, do obedience well and might be the best thing around here since canned piss. But there's a bit of a problem with helicopters. Make that a fucking *huge* problem. Hear those chopper blades at full throttle and he goes absolutely bloody troppo.'

Eather thought for a minute and then, as if he'd discovered the secret to splitting the atom: 'It's bloody noise frequency. I've heard of it before. Each dog reacts differently to noise frequency. Some can take a bird twittering, or a whistle or a siren, and pay stuff-all attention. With others they go off. With Caesar it's chopper blades cutting through the air. Nothin' to really worry about.'

I sat silently rubbing my temples. 'Do you think he'll do it in Vietnam, then?'

' 'Course he will. What do you want? An easy life?'

SOUTHERN PHUOC TUY, APRIL 1968 — PART 5

It all happened in seconds. Six black shapes hurtled towards us; the gunner lifted his feedcover and slammed on another link belt of ammunition; and I was struck in the face and body by a hot stinking gelatinous mess, temporarily blinding me. Next moment I was lifted off my feet by Mr Toad. He hoisted me with one arm and flung me aside from the trail. He grabbed Caesar's collar and threw the dog on top of me. 'Not your fight, brother.' The man was transformed from a buffoon to a professional going about his business.

It was when I rolled over to grab Caesar that a heavy black object smashed down next to me. I looked into an eye glazing over. The stench from the boar's mouth was putrid, and I gagged as the realisation hit me that we had run into a full-frontal pig attack. 'Pigs! Fucking pigs. Stop shooting!'

How could wild pigs grow so fucking enormous? Worse, these were now travelling at the speed of a charging rhino, driven mad after the wounding by the first burst of machine-gun fire. The leading half-dozen animals had been blown apart by the M60, and their entrails had air-burst, splattering up and over the leading soldiers.

'Christ, Caesar, my dog! Don't shoot my dog!' I pushed the head of the massive pig away from me—noticing how cleanly it had been severed by gunfire—and pulled the dog towards me. He was going nuts at the pandemonium around him.

Men were shrieking and calling out. Another M60 began to fire from the rear, and there was the crack-crack of automatic weapons with men trying to shoot the pigs now zipping in and out of the jungle, weaving through the hysterical New Zealanders.

When the silence came back to the jungle track I could just hear the platoon commander on the radio to company headquarters. 'Pigs. S'right, we have been attacked by a herd of pigs.' There was a hiss of static, then he spoke again: 'Negative, not Victor Charlie. Papa, india, golf. I said *fucking PIGS!*'

I could understand the communication problem: while the company commander, miles away, was readying artillery support for the 'firefight', the poor Kiwi looey was trying to tell him everything was under control. Control? What a bloody joke, I thought looking around me. The gunner was holding his head in his hands, Mr Toad was wiping blood and what looked like pig shit from his face, and Wingnut was making some effort to cover our arses in case Victor Charlie came running down the trail. 'This is like Twilight fucking Zone,' he whispered back to me.

Animals that weren't blown apart were still kicking and squealing on the ground. The trail for more than 50 yards was piles of pig blood, shit and guts, and men, shaking and speechless, beginning to drift forward to examine the astonishing scene.

I sat with my legs out straight, holding my dog. My trousers looked as if they had been hit with a buckshot of blood, and Caesar's coat glistened with a fine spray of some fluid I wasn't game to touch.

Mr Toad looked at me and gave a sigh. 'I hope the boss doesn't ask us to tidy the jungle up again.'

Sunday morning about 8am. I couldn't sleep in with all the snoring and farting in the hut. The night before Tex, Polly and Fergie had hit the city, doing the Cross. I had begged off somewhere in Paramatta and caught a cab home. The dregs had dragged themselves in, fighting and bitching, at about 6am, and now were lying about in various states of paralysis.

I was outside, smoking, when the guard sergant steered his Land Rover onto the gravel driveway towards the hut. I walked over as he pulled up.

'Private Haran?'

'Yep.'

'You got a dog called Caesar?'

'Yep.' I thought back the night before. *Was I in the shit?*

'Get your greens on, web belt and water bottle. Get your dog and your tracking equipment. Up to the guardroom a.s.a.p.'

Before I could ask why, he had accelerated away.

I didn't know Sydney all that well. I could find my way around the main RSL clubs and most big pubs, but suburban Ashfield looked much like any other suburb I'd watched flashing by during the drive into the city.

We stopped outside a corner convenience store. Police cars everywhere, coppers and people standing around with that look crowds get when they are at the centre of some public trauma or drama: open-mouthed, gawking, directionless.

WO Carter was there in greens and his bush hat. 'We've had a child abduction from outside this store. She's six or seven. The police have asked for our help to find her.'

Carter was his usual economical self, giving the whole picture in three sentences. He motioned me to follow him to a woman. It was immediately obvious this was the mother of the missing child; her face tracked with tears and the agony of total loss.

Carter turned to me and held out a pair of child's knickers. 'Treat this as a normal track from the steps of the store. A person grabbed her and walked off that way.' He pointed and then shoved the panties at me. 'Put Caesar on this.'

I buckled up the dog, thinking this would be a difficult, no, near impossible ask of an Army tracking dog. No vegetation to hold the smell, totally unfamiliar surroundings, traffic and exhaust smell everywhere, a million distractions, not the least a gaggle of rubber-necked civilians milling around near the shop.

The girl, I was informed, had left the mother's home not a hundred yards away to collect the Sunday paper and milk, a chore she had carried out many times before. As she had left the store, a man, moving quickly on foot, had snatched her up and walked off. Caesar would have to follow the scent of the girl from the panties. He'd pick up the stranger's scent too, and they'd blend. Would that confuse him? No time to fathom out the imponderables, I reckoned as I shoved the panties under Caesar's nose and shook the lead out.

He took off the moment I hissed, 'Find her, boy. *Seek.*'

We walked along the pavement like a couple out for a Sunday stroll. Me, Carter and a black dog in a tracking harness. It had to be a first for Ashfield.

No problem for one block. Crossed the street, Caesar occasionally sniffing the concrete or grass strip between footpath and road. The one thing in our favour was a time lapse of only about two hours. The smell may have drifted down and settled on the concrete in that period. Good.

Sudden turn, straight into a vacant block. Rubbish, drink cans, toilet paper, ankle-high weeds. Caesar stops at a wooden gate at block's back fence. I kick open the gate, revealing a narrow back lane. Caesar shoots forward, nose up and down, air and ground scenting. Sniff, sniff, pad, pad. He then swings from the back lane into a smaller lane heading downhill to another road. Just the click of his nails on the cement.

Shit! *Stuff it!* Straight across from me is a church with a service starting, or finishing, and there is a gathered multitude right on the bloody footpath. I tell myself to treat this as a cross-track—with 50 people crossing it.

'Excuse us, excuse us, please.' Carter did his best to clear the way, but there were still looks of bewilderment as two Army types walking a dog and half-a-dozen coppers paraded through. By now we also had a following of general public who thought this was a stunt or, maybe we were making a movie.

I was certain Caesar was holding a scent and in working mode when we turned into another side street, and I became aware of smaller houses, trees and, to my front, a cul-de-sac. I looked back and the crowd had swelled to nearly 50 people in single file, chatting, laughing or wearing looks of curiosity and concern.

We were confronted with a wide gateway, a line of bollards and behind that a large sports ground, or football oval. To the right was a parking area. Tyre marks were clearly evident in the mud, and Caesar began casting left and right, then circling back to me and forward again. He would not go on with the track.

The crowd was now gathered like spectators around a green at a golf tournament. I said to Carter that we'd lost it, or something else was going on. Caesar sat while the warrant officer examined the ground. I looked at the dog. Sure, he'd done well, but…He was looking straight across the sports ground, ears up and head forward. Was it a point? I scanned the far side of the field. A small grandstand and a concrete toilet block, I identified that through the obvious stink-pipe protruding from the roof. I pointed it out to Carter who spoke to one of the plain-clothes police.

Two young officers were dispatched to the building, and I slipped the harness over Caesar's neck. He nudged me aside and with his tongue lolling out, never taking his eyes off the toilet. A minute later there was a shout from one of the constables, and then the other emerged clutching a small figure who had her head buried in his shoulder.

It was one of those moments that stands still. You try and take stock of where you are. What time of the day is it? What are we doing here? How did we get here? Then a surge of relief, but still disbelief. Did this really happen?

The cop passed by with the little girl, and spoke quietly to me, 'She's okay. Not hurt. It's okay. That was a great job, mate.'

It seemed I'd no sooner given Caesar a drink than two arms were wrapped around his head and there was a voice speaking: 'Dear God, you hear about these things but never believe they're true.' The mother was a mix of emotions: tears, sobs, euphoria, gratitude. She got a huge wet tongue in her ear before she grabbed me, then an embarrassed Carter.

An hour later Caesar was back in his kennel, dozing, and the child was safe at home, possibly sleeping, too.

I'd left Carter talking to a newspaper reporter and snooped around asking questions of the cops. The girl had indeed been picked up by a sicko, who walked to the sports field where he had left his car parked. What his plan was then, who knows, but he locked her in the toilet before fleeing in the vehicle.

The tracking pattern Caesar had followed made sense. His track route had been the most direct from abduction site to the football ground—just as the abductor would have taken. He was trying to indicate during his last cast in the mud the abductor had been *here* and the girl was trapped over *there*. It had been a mighty effort. Even old stone-faced Carter was in awe.

I asked myself looking at him sleeping on his back with his legs stuck skyward: 'Just how bloody good are you, mate?'

SOUTHERN PHUOC TUY, APRIL 1968 — PART 6

I crawled onto the floor of the helicopter and squeezed between hesian bags full of empty waterbottles. The Kiwis had been resupplied water and a bundle of clean greens for those most devastated in the pig massacre, and I was going back to Nui Dat on the return flight. Since the pig invasion, not much had been said to me, and I didn't know if the New Zealanders were blaming me for following an animal track. I hadn't, of course; the enemy had simply used a trail which passed the biggest wild piggery in Vietnam.

No-one on the aircraft had paid much attention to me, and when I walked down the road to the kennels a bunch of guys playing volleyball hardly gave me a second look. I was grateful I didn't have to explain why almost every part of my body was covered in dry pig entrails and the dog was covered in dry blood. I had washed what I could off my face and from around the dog's eyes with what available water I had in the bush before we spent a sleepless night in ambush waiting for the VC to come back. The appalling mess dried like cardboard, and the stink was unbearable. The poor bloody animals' bowels had released at the moment they were hit by the gunfire, and almost every man in the front line had been splattered with wet faeces.

I emptied a jerry can of water over Caesar and pushed him into his run. I swear Marcus took a whiff and backed away from his mate. I stood under the shower bucket and soaped myself down. I filled two more buckets of hot water and scrubbed until it hurt. Afterwards I sat on the concrete shower floor and just stared at my feet, reliving the previous two days' events. Fergie went down to the kennels later that afternoon and soaped and rinsed Caesar.

In March, 1967 Fergie and I, along with both dogs, climbed aboard a Land Rover for the ride to Richmond Air Base. After an uneventful flight to Brisbane, we unpacked our belongings in a run-down hut—identical to the derelict World War II model accommodation at Ingleburn. This was Enoggera, home to the 2nd Battalion, the Royal Australian Regiment, nearly a 1000 men in the final throes of training for a year in Vietnam. We joined Support Company, which controlled the Tracking Team, but the day we arrived most of the men we would be working with were away on exercise in north Queensland.

There was no time to catch our breath or dwell on Vietnam, the war, or departure date. We were both sent on pre-embarkation leave and I went back to Adelaide for a week while Fergie motored home to Redcliffe, just outside Brisbane.

Back from leave, we went through final pre-embarkation checks and were told we were on the 2nd Battalion Advance Party to Vietnam. We would fly ahead of the main battalion, which would sail on the HMAS *Sydney* and arrive in Vietnam two weeks later. This, we worked out, would give the dogs plenty of time to acclimatise in Vietnam. We also figured dogs couldn't sail on the old aircraft carrier.

'Maybe they think they'll go overboard,' said Fergie.

'Maybe they don't know where dogs could have a shit?' I suggested.

I had been a Tracker in training for not quite a year. I was now a Tracker readying for real war. But I could think no further ahead than the flight to Saigon.

On 7 May, we put the dogs in specially-prepared travelling crates and watched them lifted on board the big RAAF Hercules. Fergie and I climbed in behind them, made ourselves as comfortable as we could on the nylon strap seats, and watched as the rear door went up. Looking back along the piles of crates and slung-down materiel of war, I glimpsed two sets of yellow eyes looking through the front grill on the dog crates.

'On our way, fellas. Have a sleep, and no crapping in there.'

We dozed but sleep wouldn't come in the icy-cold main fuselage. I stuck my head in the cockpit to see the co-pilot with his feet up reading a book. Ahead was a blue sky of the most breathtaking beauty I had ever seen. The pilot pointed down to the coast of Australia, faded brown and splashes of green, gradually drifting behind us. We touched down that night at Butterworth air base near Penang, our first taste and smell of Asia, but we were all so exhausted the strange environment hardly registered.

Next morning early we took off for Vietnam.

Good Morning Saigon

The Hercules C-130 lumbered onto the concrete apron at Tan Son Nhut, and its four big engines shut down with a shudder. The rear ramp dropped and we walked out into the wall of heat, stink and noise of Vietnam.

Fergie and I recovered the dogs from their travelling crates and took them for a relief walk. Hygiene and good taste usually dictated we find a clear area to defecate. First problem after arriving in the war zone: where do dogs shit? It seemed like no specific crap area existed at Saigon airport, a chaos of aircraft and a thousand bodies moving like ghosts through the haze and pollution.

A plane took off and landed every 45 seconds. Hercs, Caribous, massive Starlifters, jet fighters and even outdated propeller-driven fossils. There was also the clatter and whine of the greatest concentration of choppers in the world: the war workhorse, the Iroquois; gunships, including the jet-powered Cobra; reconnaissance choppers, the Kiowa and Cheyenne; and the 'hillclimber', the Chinook, capable of moving a whole platoon.

The stink of aviation fuel and the fetid smell of rotten vegetables coming from the fenceline made concealing two dogs shitting seem stupidly irrelevant.

Inside the airbase's cyclone fence, with its single straggly strand of barbed wire, were the sounds of machinery going to war. Outside the fence I took my first curious gawk at the passing parade of civilian life; midafternoon in Saigon. A woman in a conical hat sat in the gutter and stared at the dogs, then she looked at me. Was it cold indifference, or was it war fatigue? A blur of trishaws obscured her for a moment, then she was there again, now fanning herself with her hat, hair pulled severely back into a bun. A smile spread across her face as Caesar lifted his leg. I caught a glimpse of a line of teeth reddened with betel juice. A fleet of Lamborettas, and she was gone.

We hauled our webbing, hold-alls and rifles over to the closest building with an Australian flag, Air Dispatch, and leaned against the wall. Talk was virtually impossible with the noise generated on the airfields. It alternated between the clatter and thud of the choppers to the howl of a Phantom's afterburner, curving black smoke trailing a dirty fuselage that gradually became a black dot on the horizon. The background noise was engines at high rev or winding down and taxiing in, spent after a day dumping their loads somewhere Out There.

'What a freaky li'l fucker!'

Startled at the words behind me, I swung around to be faced by two black soldiers. One was a super-tall, basketballer build, who wore his green fatigues over a wiry frame. An enormous grin spread across a face as black as charcoal. The other man was short, heavily built, unsmiling and mean-looking, with his hands shoved down into his pockets. Both had a collection of beads around their necks.

'This yo' dog, man?' The basketballer was down on his haunches patting Caesar.

'Wha's yo' dog do, man?'

'Um, he's a tracking dog,' I replied. 'He…'

'No *shi-it*, he chase Charlie?' The big guy stood up. 'How much time you got, man?'

I stupidly looked at my watch.

'Naw, man. How much time you got left in the 'Nam? How short you?'

'Oh, we just got here.'

Both men buckled at the waist, laughing.

'No one got that much time in this sorry fuckin' place.'

The shorter soldier gave me a quiet, hard look. 'Yo' mean yo' dog ain't caught no gooks yet?'

'No, we haven't been out in the jungle yet.' I was beginning to feel stupid.

The two just looked at each other. Then the grin came back to basketballer's face. 'Lis'n, we gotta go. We short, an' soon on tha' Freedom Bird. When yo' dog catch Charlie make sure he bite his ass.'

A few paces away the short one turned back. 'But you make sure Charlie don' get yo' dog first or he'll eat him!' Both men laughed, slapping each other on the back. I felt a slow depression come over me.

Our first encounter with two different cultures—one black, the other Asian. One was sick humour, the other was enigmatic.

The air-dispatch sergeant appeared. 'Two personnel and engineers stores to Nui Dat.'

Caesar and Marcus had no official Army designation in 1967. The category of 'Dog' did not exist. So on the manifest they appeared as 'engineers stores', along with barbed wire, picks, shovels, C4 explosive and bulldozers.

'Over here,' said Fergie.

The dispatcher glanced down at his clipboard. 'You're on Wallaby Airlines, 1425 hours.'

'No bull, we've got our own airline over here?' said a surprised Fergie.

The dispatcher looked at him like something stuck to his shoe. 'No, dumbshit. Wallaby Airlines is the Caribou taking you to Phuoc Tuy, Nui Dat, right? It's not a bloody airline; it's the RAAF. Bay nine, don't miss it.'

By the time we got into the back of the Caribou our jungle greens were saturated with sweat. The loadmaster told us to put our rifles on the deck, or barrels down if we had to hold them 'so you don't shoot the top out the bloody airplane', then secured for take-off. The dogs slumped on the floor, looking as sick as we were of military aircraft. Two engines coughed and barked into life with a gush of black smoke, and the Caribou weaved and wobbled onto the runway.

There were six or seven other bodies on board, slumped back in the bench seats which were basically webbing and aluminium struts. Thankfully it wasn't as freezing as the Herc, which we'd heard had popped a ramp gasket bringing Cassius and Justin up months earlier, filling the fuselage with a freezing mist.

Five minutes into the flight and Marcus was on alert as a digger opposite chewed into a chocolate Hershey bar. Another digger, returning from leave and looking wasted from a week in an Asian fleshpot, unwrapped chewing gum and passed it over. He looked at the dogs and then at us.

'What they for?'

'Trackers,' I said. 'Following up enemy after contact. We're with 2RAR.'

The soldier stopped chewing and looked at me without changing his expression. 'You gotta be bloody jokin', right? *Tracking* the bloody Nogs? Don't need to bloody *track* Charlie, mate. The Nogs'll come and find you, no fuckin' worries.'

After the comments from the two black soldiers, the fellow digger's remarks sent me further down the we-are-stuffed scale. We all shut up while the Caribou droned south towards touchdown at Luscombe Field, Nui Dat, the home of the Australian Task Force in Vietnam, and our official start of the war.

Combatants talk in shorthand. You could be six or 12 months in country and have virtually no meaningful conversation with a mate. In the bush, words were spoken with economy, mumbled or transmitted in hushed whispers to another man or on the 25-set radio. Sometimes it was just hand signals: trail or river ahead, stop, move forward and thumbs down—Enemy.

There was also a priority list of questions when you met a grunt for the first time. First question: How much time you got? Second: When you last get some pussy? Third: Where you from? All other information sucked. After the priority questionnaire, conversation still didn't progress much more past a situation update. This was the way it was with the gaggle of men I had hunkered down with when we arrived at the 3/5 Cavalry.

'Ah got a brother in the war, down in the Delta...'

'Ah had a cousin in the war. Got kilt in the DMZ...'

'Mah ol' lady's layin' some other guy back home...'

'I could use some cool shit...'

'Where you from in Australia...?'

'Wha's your dog's name...?'

A request comes over AFVN Radio: 'That's Hendrix. I dig Hendrix. You dig Hendrix...?'

Cleaning House

I sat in a tent surrounded by sandbags—a blast wall against exploding shells. A bare lightbulb, specked with dead mozzies indicated illuminated habitation for the next 12 months. A floor made from deconstructed duckboards sat on shell casings. In the middle of the four-man tent stood a table, knocked together from odd planks of wood and covered with a badly soiled Army-issue blanket. I imagined the previous occupants playing cards and writing letters at that table. There was a scorch mark in the middle where someone had tried to cook food or brew coffee on a hexamine stove, and there was a crushed confectionery tin doubling as an ashtray.

Three Army cots were pushed into opposite corners. Above each were suspended worn, Nui Dat dust-stained mosquito nets. Shelves, hammered together from what I guessed were mortar or artillery shell boxes, leaned crazily against one sandbagged wall. Next to those was a solitary rusted steel locker to hang clothes. Two fold-up chairs almost completed the depression.

The tent stank of decay, mildew. Some of the sandbags had burst and were bleeding red sludge onto the floor. In places the flysheet over the main tent had broken loose and sagged. At the foot of my cot I had thrown my webbing, backpack and hold-all, and now I placed my rifle on the table and began to strip it down. I thought best to get down and do something; familiar routine would refocus the mind from the mess.

Fergie was sitting on his cot looking at the floor. 'Soon have this looking like home, you watch,' he said, stamping down hard at something crawling between the duckboards.

An hour before we had walked Caesar and Marcus up to their kennels. They had been built in preparation for our coming by the engineers and, like anything the sappers constructed, would withstand a Force 10 and an eight on the Richter scale at the same time.

I opened the gate with a grunt. 'A bloody water buffalo wouldn't get out of here.'

The two kennels were identical to those back at Ingleburn, but the main supports and cross-members looked as though they had been used making the main Sydney wharf. The cement floor was grey with newness, freshly trowelled and smooth as glass. Out the back the engineers had built a drain to take stormwater and the run-off from scrubbing out.

'Somebody got something right. Better than the shithole we've got.' Fergie let Marcus sniff about in the kennel before we took both dogs for a run through their new environment. They bounded around the rubber trees, making every trunk a pee stop, and checked out the knee-high ferns and piles of rubber tree leaves. It was a million new smells; dog heaven.

The first few days at the Task Force Base, Nui Dat, were spent working like beavers cleaning out our tent, refilling sandbags to replace the rotting ones on the blast wall and stringing new mossy nets. Fergie acquired a shade for the light, and I scrounged a new blanket for the table. I repaired the washstand outside the tent and nailed my new stainless-steel mirror to the tree above the plastic washbasin. The mirror came from a beautiful leather-bound shaving kit that my mother and father had given me during pre-embarkation leave.

I recalled my father's parting words as I left to go to war.

Suspended in anticipation of some profound words of wisdom and advice, my old man said: 'Don't forget to wash the soap out of the shaving brush. If you don't, it'll go hard and become useless.'

My mother said she'd send some cake.

I dismantled another mortar box and repaired the shelves. Fergie put his paperbacks along one shelf, and I stuck my collection of James Bond on the other. Maybe it was training, perhaps even motivation to take back territory from the rats and roaches. In any event, it was standard digger mentality to turn any place into livable space, be it the brick lines of Kapooka, the weatherboard at Inf. Centre, a weapon pit in the bush or in the red muck-impregnated tents at Nui Dat, Phuoc Tuy province. It also killed time waiting for the rest of the battalion to arrive.

On 30 May 1967 a troopship dropped anchor at Vung Tau, and slicks of Chinooks began ferrying the main force of 2RAR to Nui Dat. The 6th Battalion was carried out to the ship on the return journeys. A thousand men hardly brushed shoulders, hardly exchanged a word as the switch took place.

That afternoon the rest of the Tracking Team, part of the Anti-Tank Platoon, moved into half-a-dozen tents in the Support Company.

XA BANG, PHUOC TUY PROVINCE, FIRE SUPPORT BASE, 1967

I was squatting under a single plastic sheet called a hootchie. It was taped to a shovel on one side and a steel stake on the other. My knees were drawn up under my chin and I was staring out past the wire to the distant tree line which was gradually disappearing behind sheets of rain. The wretchedness of the situation was only compounded by a dog who alternately shoved his nose or arse into my face while trying to contract himself to his smallest size to avoid the rain cascading over the side of the hootchie. I was doing the same. It was a personal struggle to squeeze into the driest spot in six square feet of dry earth. Not 50 yards away Fergie was doing the same with a much bigger dog. Fergie was smaller than me, but Marcus was bigger than Caesar, so I suppose it evened out to the same battle for space.

'Call yourself a bloody war dog, bloody hard Australian sheep dog, tough-as-hell labrador who loves the wet? Piss off outside.'

The dog looked at me with contempt. He retreated further under the plastic shelter like a moray eel into a hole, mouth half open, challenging me. I pushed my body into his and he placed his back legs across my stomach, effectively pinning me down. I saw red and shoved at him, missed and rolled out into the mud. Staggering up I stepped on my rifle and tripped over my webbing, bringing the plastic sheet down over the dog.

Caesar panicked and tried to run, dragging the hootchie with him. Cursing and spitting water out of my mouth, I slithered in pursuit after dog and possessions. Twiggy and Thatch watched chuckling from under their perfectly strung shelters, where mugs collected rainwater and every piece of equipment was bone dry. Twiggy was cackling and squinting. 'Mistreat that dog again, mister, and we'll fuckin' report you to the RSPCA.'

WALK IN THE FOREST

Operation Barossa was a day-out walk in the forest for the Tracking Team. Specifically, a patrol through a disused rubber plantation called Binh Ba. At 0800 hours we lined up in chalks on the side of Luscombe Field as the American Assault Helicopter Company touched down.

They came sitting on their tails, then tilted and bumped forward. It was an adrenaline rush, the battalion's first full-scale airlift in the war zone. Marshalls with orange waistcoats waved us aboard, and Caesar was already in the throes of another wobbly—but I was ready for him, clamped down hard on his lead and collar to prevent the high jump, and made a run for it. *Crunch* into a pile of packs, men and rifles on the floor, grab for a hand-hold, any hand-hold, and then we were rising. No doors on the Vietnam chopper, real door-gunners—black visors pushed up, hunched over twin M60s—and just the whip of wind and a sharp lurch as we turned north for Binh Ba.

In just minutes we were in descent and touchdown on an old airstrip. Thump and jolt, drag the dog clear and flatten in the low grass. Weapon up, pointing out, and backpack flies forward, almost dislocating the neck.

This was an acclimatisation and orientation operation—your equivalent of a day trip and sight-see in Phuoc Tuy province. Trackers would travel with the Battalion HQ, strung out in open-file formation for a quiet walk through the rubber.

Among those who swore while they swung packs and hoisted ammunition belts was Simon, solidly built six-footer, Pancho Villa moustache and bush hat pulled forward shadowing his face. The visual tracker could have been the original wild man who walked out of the jungles of Borneo. He slung an M79 grenade launcher over one shoulder and carried spare bombs in two bandoliers. Not one to be shy about self-preservation, Simon also carried his SLR (self-loading rifle) and a personal weapon—a powerful six-shot Python .357 Magnum. He took criticism of his arsenal with 'Don't run up looking for me when you're getting your arse shot off.' Simon had a black belt in judo, and had a disconcerting habit of lashing out with a vicious elbow chop when awoken from a deep sleep. This usually happened when it was his turn for sentry duty, or night picket.

'Sure as shit, if he does that again I'll put a fucking machete in his head,' said Blue, another Army redhead, tough as teak but good-natured enough to smile after a death threat. He carried two belts of link ammo over each shoulder and backed up Thatch, who was carrying one of the platoon's two M60 General Purpose Machine Guns. The main firepower of the infantry section was the '60, which was fitted with a bipod and could be mounted on a tripod. It was called the Gun, the '60 or, by the Americans, the Pig. Thatch came from the Northern Territory, and if you'd ever seen a young bloke on a back road leaning against a ute while he knocked the dust from his hat, you'd have seen Thatch. Preparing for his trek through the trees, the Territorian looked like a Mexican bandit with two bandoliers across his chest.

To his left, pulling on a last-minute rollie, was JC, or Joe, who was good friends with Thatch. Tall, lopey, with nut-brown skin and a face seasoned by the wind and sun of Esperance, slow-talking Joe concealed a deep intellect and appreciation for the good things in life. He already had acquired a GI double-pocket shirt, and packed belt ammo across the back of his pack.

Behind was Twiggy, Trackers' comedian, who told jokes with a squint in one eye. A National Serviceman, or Nasho, Twiggy constantly reminded the Regs what shitwits they were. He was a coverman for the visual trackers or the dog handlers.

Les was the sort of soldier who would go unnoticed in the team. He was a dog handler's coverman and, like Marcus's handler Fergie, almost vanished under the load he carried.

Schoolteacher Ken, a Nasho, was coverman to Fergie and Marcus. He was separated at birth from Simon and reunited for a tour of Vietnam, so the joke went. The pair were almost identical, down to the facial hair.

The command structure included Corporal Bill. He was quiet, and walked everywhere on the base with a clipboard under his arm. He told me: 'It makes you look busy when you've got nothing to do. Bullshit always baffles brains.'

The other tracker corporal was Bob, another Queenslander who had only just earned his stripes. The young, strongly-built non-commissioned officer, or NCO, was an accomplished visual tracker and map reader. He would be team leader of the tracking unit which comprised Caesar and I, gunner Thatch and coverman Les. But the combat tracking team and the two dogs were interchangeable; we could slip into each other's place if the situation demanded.

The trackers in each battalion were joined at the hip to the Anti-Tank component of the platoon. The VC weren't big on tanks, so the Anti-Tankers were stripped of their beloved 106s, tank busters and, as some small compensation, now lugged the super-lightweight M72 rocket launcher bunker busters, which extended into a mini-bazooka. Fire the rocket and you simply threw away the empty tube. M72s also had been issued to all the rifle companies as the frequency of bunker-system fighting became more apparent.

Vietnam was the testing ground for a staggering assortment of new weapons and equipment, all designed to up the body count with maximum bang for the buck. New types of bombs and grenades; faster fire rates; lighter armaments; quicker combat vehicles bristling with cannon; illumination flares that turned night into yellow and white strobe; and ordnance which was chocked with flechette, canister and white phosphorous. Primitive country, futuristic war games.

By the time we reached the limit of Binh Ba we were stuffed, the dogs were cranky and my back was killing me. It had been three hours of walking in the shade, but the sweat was already stinging the hell out of bloody chafes around my hips and shoulders. With a clatter and thud the choppers touched down, Caesar went ballistic and we went home.

It was early morning, and I was lying under my hootchie swirling the dregs of coffee in a mug while Caesar was scratching behind his ear. From some distance behind me a conversation between two diggers carried down. 'You're always taking my jam. What am I supposed to put on my biscuits?'

'Vegemite. You reckon you love Vegemite, and I hate the shit. I've got the jam, you've got the Vegemite.'

'But I want jam. I feel like jam. Gimme my fucking jam back.'

'Right, have your shitty jam back...and make your own bloody brew this time. It's the last time I make a brew for you, prickhead.'

'Don't prick me, mate. Don't you bloody prick me. I made the last five bloody brews for you. And all I asked for was jam for my crackers. Just this one time and you crack a shitty.'

'Hey! Don't push me, or I'll fuckin' well thump you. Gimme the jam and fuck off.'

'Okay, okay, have the jam and take the bloody Vegemite and stick your brews up your arse.'

Saddling Up

Two weeks into the tour and we still hadn't had a job. I took the opportunity to do something about the pain factor, reorganising my equipment after we had done two operations for further acclimatisation and orientation. It had been a pain in the arse, and every other part of the body. I wondered why they called 12 months in a war a *tour*. A tour indicated passports, guides, beer and room service—pleasure. Vietnam was to date hips and shoulders rubbed raw, oppressive heat and raking up rubber leaves at Nui Dat.

We had done a short run to Vung Tau to get Caesar and Marcus checked by the US vet, and I had traded a set of imitation brass RAR shoulder tags for a fibreglass backpack frame. The Yank who gave it to me said a LRRP had given it to him. A LRRP was a Long Range Reconnaissance Patrol operative, and *We Deal In Death* was their motto. They went out for days, weeks, and came back with a collection of ears.

Wondering about the history of the last bloke who owned it, I strapped my backpack to the frame and taped foam to the lower strut. I slung it for a fit and figured it would stop me being cut in half after the first two or three miles. Comfort in the scrub was now an obsession. Fergie and the other trackers were also making some urgent readjustments.

We had been split into two teams and placed on Ready Reaction status, which meant we had to be at the chopper pad in 10 minutes when the call came. Marcus and Caesar would alternate on call-outs. I was first up, so I began to pack.

Food: three days' rations, a mix of US three-day packs and Australian one-day packs. That gave a combination including canned meatballs in sauce, a spongy omelette or two,

American pound cake, pork and beans and turkey loaf. Along with that was a boring mixture of biscuits, cheese, jams and rice. There was a variety of fruit in cans from peaches to pears and the favourite, fruit cocktail.

Coffee in bulk, sugar in bulk, a tube of condensed milk, a toilet roll and at least a week's worth of cigarettes, usually heavy menthol such as Salem or Winston. They helped soothe the nerves and keep the mozzies away from your face.

Condiments and luxuries: a can of chocolate for hot drinks, chocolate bars for an energy hit, a packet of curry to kill the taste of everything, a small bottle of Worcestershire Sauce to make sure it was dead. Essential was a small jar of Vegemite. After pulling all that together, cull it, throw the biscuits out and pack in more smokes and chewing gum.

The dog: five cans of American dog food, five packets of hard biscuits and a brush and comb. I put a plastic bottle of military-issue insect repellent in with that; it would strip paint but keep the bugs off.

Sleeping gear was a silk sheet and a single, plastic one-man shelter. Two pairs of spare socks. No underclothes needed.

Firepower: two fragmentation grenades, 12 Armalite magazines with 18 rounds each, every fourth round a tracer bullet. Small bottle of oil and a cleaning cloth. They went into two basic pouches on the webbing belt, along with a roll of black tape. Black plastic insulation tape was the most valuable item a soldier could carry after his rifle; black tape held the war effort together. I sheathed the M16 bayonet— it wasn't for close-contact use but supported my steel mug over a flame when making coffee.

Heat was provided not by the useless hexamine blocks, but a pebble-size lump of C4 explosive broken from a block which had been scrounged from the Assault Pioneers. Stick a match in that small amount of plastic explosive and water was boiling in 15 seconds. Stick a detonator in the full block and you'd shift a house. Highly illegal, but a necessary practice for the grunt in the field, soaking wet and hanging out for a caffeine hit.

Next, six water bottles: three on the belt and three attached to the backpack. Metal mugs were folded and clamped onto three of the bottles, one for Caesar's personal use, my coffee mug and one for cooking. I carried a small dixie, an aluminium dish, for the dog to eat from. Don't forget the can-opener, which doubled as a spoon.

I packed the lot up. Simon and Ken offered to carry two cans of dog food, which I happily passed on. I knew the trackers also carried extra water for the dogs. They never told me, but I knew they had it; tough guys, but pussies when it came to kids and animals.

On the tent table I stripped, oiled and reassembled the Armalite, checked the firing mechanism and daubed green paint over the black stock to remove the shine. Next, I strapped a shell dressing to the butt with black tape. Another digger would rip that off and put it on me if I lost a lump of flesh. I'd do the same for him. The rifle was the lightest part of all the gear I carried.

Now all I had to do was get this lot up and on my back. Walking with the full load was nearly bloody impossible. I wobbled and staggered until I got up a sort of slow trot. Stop and I'd fall on my arse. Walking through the 'j' was tortuous; you snagged every branch and fell over every log. Simon, after the first two ops, said: 'You travel through the "j" under inertia or under your own momentum. If you stop, sit down or kneel.'

I asked him to try doing that with a dog on a lead. I had grizzled and whinged about this back at the Tracking Wing back home, where Carter and French had assured us all it wouldn't happen.

'Naw,' said Armidale Tex one night when we had been speculating on the war. 'We'll be sittin' back there wanking ourselves and they'll give us a call. Out we'll go and brass up a VC. Back to camp and back to suckin' on piss.' Tex stood up and laughed. 'Yeah, right. Fucking bullshit, crap and corruption.'

A day after I had got myself ready for the real thing, the real thing happened. The shout came down the lines: 'Trackers out!'

LONG KANH PROVINCE, 1968

I was spooning meat from a can onto Caesar's plate when Fergie came walking over with Marcus. The dog handler simply sat down and stared at the dog food. Marcus dutifully sat next to his master making whining sounds while watching his mate eat his tea.

'What's up with you? You look sick.' I offered Fergie a fruit cocktail or a brew. We were on a fire support base, there was a lot of shit happening all over the place but we hadn't done a track from here yet.

Fergie spat on the ground. 'I *am* sick, but not as crook as I mighta been. You won't believe what happened to me this morning. Some corporal fuckwit comes by and tells me I'm going out as a scout on a recce patrol. No dog, just me. I saddle up and say no problem, right? Then he comes back and says sorry he didn't realise I might have to go out and track so he grabs some other poor bugger to scout for his patrol, right?'

I nodded. Dog handlers were routinely called on to scout for patrols.

'Well,' Fergie continued, his eyes going wet, 'wouldn't you bloody know it, the bastard who took my place is in hospital with no legs. Stepped on a fucking jumping jack.'

For a few moments we shared the silence of the blessed; those who were in the right place at the wrong time.

In Harness

Four of us in a Land Rover made Eagle Farm in minutes. After Luscombe Field, it was the central helicopter pick-up point for 2RAR inside Nui Dat. The Huey came clattering in, banked sharply and thumped down. Caesar frothed and spun, and I climbed into the main seat while the other three men spread across the floor. It was a matter of seconds and the chopper was lifting across Nui Dat hill, over the main rubber, and the red and brown shades of 1ATF turned to jungle green.

The pilots climbed, and cool air washed through the aircraft. We headed south, then swung east. Below, bomb craters full of rainwater winked up as the sunlight splashed over them. Now paddis, bamboo, thick bush, then a double canopy of forest reaching several hundred feet or more. This is what the diggers called 'the j' or 'the scrub', the Americans called it 'the boonies'. In any language it was tiger country— enemy territory.

He was called Victor Charlie, radio phonetics for VC or the Viet Cong. He was out here, probably with the regional enemy main force, D445 Battalion. His Big Brothers were the National Liberation Front with the 274th NVA Regiment—professionals tooled up with AK-47s and RPGs. Mention of the NVA caused an anal tightening. They were fully equipped and trained to fight and hold ground. The VC ranged from the peasant with a rifle to the hard-core guerilla with a machine-gun who knew the local patch. The NVA were reinforced from the North, disciplined, and had bloodied noses in more than one bout with the American forces. Know your enemy.

The chopper suddenly banked and skimmed at treetop level. A shuddering turn, and then a clearing with purple smoke billowing up as our landing marker.

The Iroquois was gone by the time we entered the trees. Team commander Bob had a quick talk with the platoon commander and came back. 'A bunch of Nogs walked in to the platoon while they were sitting having a smoke. Seems the forward scout was on alert and brassed up one of the VC. Three others, at least, took off. There's a good showing of blood, so the looey thought he'd give it a go...So let's go.'

We dropped our heavy backpacks with platoon head-quarters, and a follow-up section of men moved in behind us while I harnessed up Caesar in double time. There was no need for a visual inspection to find sign—I was looking straight down at real, bright-red blood on the foot track that wound off into the gloom.

My mouth was so dry with the tension I could hardly say '*Seek!*' But Caesar didn't need much encouragement—he took off like a rocket, then braked for his obligatory pee.

A year or more of training, obedience, lectures, Bulli and Helensburgh and I was on a live track. I wanted to stop and do a check that we had everything right. *Couldn't we have coffee and chat first?* The air insertion and deployment had been breathtakingly quick. I had looked at the Delta Company diggers, there were hard looks that said: *We just shot Charlie and the bastards are still all around the fucking place. Don't fuck up. Anything, but don't fuck this up.*

We were on a well-used foot trail and the blood gave confirmation we were on the scent. At one stage I thought I detected a piece of gut or intestine and I heaved. Caesar trotted forward, nose up and down like a vacuum cleaner. Bob covered me, his SLR almost at his shoulder for a fast shot. Ken was next, to the left, and the section commander had moved an M60 right up behind the three of us, but I got no comfort out of the available firepower. Every sense in me reached out for sound, smell and a possible point. Then my world went upside down and I fell into a hole.

Bob crashed down, rifle at the ready, and a message was whispered back: 'The dog handler's just fell in a hole.'

It was four feet deep and as a long as a grave. I pulled myself up and noticed I was just off the foot track. The vegetation had concealed the fact it was here, but I knew why it was there the moment I looked back at the soldiers: I was standing in a VC weapon pit that had clear fire straight down the trail. We were next to a camp or a bunker complex, and a sentry would normally be in this hole.

I scrambled out and gave Bob the thumbs down field signal. Enemy! Where was Caesar? He was sitting in the middle of the track looking straight ahead, ears up.

Where had I seen that before? Ashfield, Sydney? A sports-ground? A toilet block? A little girl lost? I calmly reeled in the tracking trace and whispered to Bob. 'Bunkers, gotta be bunkers, or a VC camp.'

Bob crept forward while I covered him and Ken covered the left flank. The machine-gunner knew his stuff, he moved to the right.

'Can't see a thing. You better go on and see if you get a point,' Bob hissed at me, never taking his eyes of the foot track.

I moved up, shortened the tracking lead. *'Get 'em, boy.'*

About 50 yards later Caesar pointed. I could see ahead what looked like a white shroud lying on the ground. It rippled as if by a breeze then a thousand white butterflies lifted off the man's body. A minute later I was looking down at my first dead VC.

It had been two kilometres and we had tracked into a bunker system. Appearing as low anthills in the jungle, VC bunkers were engineering marvels, albeit deathtraps, that sucked in sections, platoons, companies and chopped them to pieces. We had heard of those that were a mile long and just as wide; complex, multi-level subterranean towns and small cities with operating theatres, lecture rooms, a criss-crossing, booby-trapped maze of tunnels and spider holes where a trapdoor flew back and advancing troops were sprayed with automatic fire along predetermined firelanes.

During dog training we had heard next to nothing about bunker complexes; Vietnam was a lot of on-the-job training. But I had been worded-in by a couple of soldiers from the 101 Airborne in Vung Tau, who spoke about the monsters around Saigon, Cu Chi, the Iron Triangle, War Zone D— places that had a ring of blood and thunder, thanks to the bunker systems that had been under construction years ago while the French were still fighting their little war.

Here we were, right in one. I was walking backwards, eyes fixed on the silent anthills with narrow-slitted mouths, topped by three feet of overhead cover and leaves, invisible from the air, almost invisible from ground level.

I took one last look at the dead man. There was no eventual peace in death and war. Twisted and contorted like an earthquake had gone off inside him, the guerilla had caught the burst of the Aussie forward scout full on, and his last moment of life was one of shock and surprise. His comrades had carried him as far as the camp and dropped him. I felt a guilty moment of disappointment over our first track...and the pursued had died on us.

There was a sense of urgency. The VC bunker complex had to be given a quick search, the dead soldier pulled over with toggle ropes and buried, and ambushes had to be laid on the tracks entering and exiting the huge camp system. Time was tight, with only an hour or so of light left under the forest canopy. All the time there was the threat VC would mount a counterattack; it was unlikely he would allow ground to be taken without exacting a price.

The three platoons, just under 100 men, moved quickly up the trail from the chopper site. Three disgruntled soldiers were carrying our packs and shooting black looks all round. 'Thanks a bloody lot for nothin', mate.' Shaking and grunting with exertion, the digger threw my pack down and stormed off to find his section. I thought I'd be shitty myself, lugging some other bastard's load.

The trackers were stuck for the night with the rifle company, and we had to rapidly adjust to normal disciplined soldiering in the bush. We retreated with the company HQ and a platoon back from the bunkers about 200 yards and went into a night-defensive position, known as a harbour. There was a flurry of radio activity while the company commander organised an engineer team to be flown in at first light to blow the complex. The forward artillery observer, or FO, laid fire missions for artillery support if it was needed, and the two platoon commanders who had been assigned ambushes were briefed. The officer commanding, or OC, put two platoons up to ambush entry and exit tracks and held one back in depth as HQ protection.

If the VC came back in the dark they would use one of the two tracks and trigger an ambush. If they then bolted, or called up reinforcements, the artillery was now laid and the big 105 guns at the Horseshoe Fire Base near Nui Dat would fire up and hammer any area around our positions.

Darkness in the jungle comes without twilight shadow.

One moment there is light striking the trees, the next only the glimmer of an illuminated watch is visible in total blackness.

A harbour involves the three machine-guns placed at 12, four and eight o'clock. Nylon cord is run around the perimeter joining the guns, and soldiers take turns doing piquet, or gun sentry. Hold the cord and walk around, placing one foot in front of the other, like a blind man feeling his way along a wall. One hour or two staring into the coalpit, creep back and wake up your relief, and so on through the night the ritual is repeated. In an ambush there is no movement, one man usually shakes the soldier awake who is next to him. Dozing off in a harbour and missing a gun shift was a chargeable offence. Sleeping in an ambush was chargeable, and suicidal.

Switching from day routine to night routine was done quietly and methodically; hours of practice during infantry training, and I completed my own preparations quickly.

With no prospect of rain, I spread my plastic shelter on the ground and threw my sleeping silk on top of that. My webbing, pack and Armalite were laid alongside the sleeping gear. Earlier I had wolfed down a cold tea of biscuits, cheese and jam and managed a quick brew. While I cleaned my rifle, Bob kept watch to the front. Ken covered for Bob as he cleaned his weapon, while I fed the dog from his steel dixie. He ate quickly and I walked him over to the machine-gun and forward of it so he could defecate outside the perimeter. I remained in sight of the gunner, who watched me while he sipped his tea. Next, I smeared repellent on my face and hands and stood-to as a four-man clearing patrol quietly circled our position.

Night came like someone turned the lights out. Not for

Caesar, though. The blue or yellow glare you see in a dog's eye when a light is shone on the animal at night is called the tapetum. This is a membrane surrounding the retina in a canine's eye, and is the secret to a dog's ability to see well in the dark. The tapetum reflects light towards the retina twice, giving the dog two chances to capture an image we as humans only get once. The dog's eye has more rods than cones, unlike humans; rods pick up dim light, cones are the colour receptors. So, dogs see better at night than us, but are not so good in the vision department in the bright light of day. Dogs are not totally colour blind, but do have poor colour perception. Their world is mainly black, white and grey with some shades of orange.

I tied Caesar to my ankle, and rolled in the silk. Sleep came instantly.

There was an explosion but no shock of impact or detonation. I sat bolt up in the dark. Shit, I've been blinded by an incoming shell. The blackness in the jungle at night was suffocating; you could feel it touching you. I ran my hands over my face and pressed my thumbs into my eyes. Just flashes again. I held my watch up and felt a rush of relief at the luminosity on the dials. I hadn't been hit by anything. My hand instinctively went down to the leather strap which attached the dog to my boot while sleeping at night in the forest. No strap. No dog. Shit, the Nogs have crept inside our perimeter and stolen my dog. There were no rational thoughts in the moments after waking in the jungle at night, just confusion and disorientation.

I fought to grasp back discipline and clear thought. I reached down my left side for the Armalite and spoke softly into the pitch black 'Caesar, come boy. Come!'

No panting or sound of waking from the war dog. He had

definitely shot through. He never did this, never tried to leave my side. If he had gone outside the perimeter and tried to come back in near the machine-gun, which was manned, he'd be shot for bloody sure. God, we'd shoot the tracking dog. My dog. He'd be dead and I'd be charged. Court-martialled? What do you get for causing death of an Army dog by neglect?

A hand grabbed my shoulder. 'That you, Pete?'

A soldier had felt his way around the perimeter from the gun position, bumping awake every other poor sod.

'I've got Caesar here. He just trotted up to the gun then went out in front of us for a shit.'

'Good manners, but scared the fuck out of us.'

Maybe I later woke in anticipation of being shaken up to do gun piquet, but I was now sitting up and reaching into the blackness for my weapon, and the dog was bolt upright next to me just as one of the rifle platoons sprung its ambush.

There were 'Shits!' and 'Bugger its!' from all round the perimeter as every man rolled out of his bedding and into a fire position. The clatter of two M60s and exploding Claymore mines came from 500 yards away, but it sounded like it was happening behind the closest tree, so still was the night. A crackle of radio transmission and the first spotting artillery round came over like a freight train.

Shells exploding in the jungle at night sound like a door slamming in a fierce wind. The FO had called a marker shot, and now the platoon commander in the ambush position was radioing where he wanted the next round, gauging distance from his location to the blast by the white flash of the explosion and how much shrapnel was slapping the trees around him. Another thump back at the fire base and the freight train of artillery came once again. *Blam!*

The round was where the platoon wanted it, and the instruction was given to fire for effect. The enemy was now under a barrage of 105 shells that ripped into the forest. Those who had fled the ambush, if any had, were being blown apart. The last thing they would hear was the freight train whistle as the shells came in.

In 30 minutes the fight was over. Light would reveal the dead and damage. For the remaining hours until sunrise, Caesar and I lay and listened to our breathing.

Three VC were killed in the ambush and a few hundred square yards of prime jungle was laid waste.

The Tracking Team moved back to the clearing soon after first light. We climbed on board the Huey, while the sappers, with half a dozen boxes of explosives, offloaded for the walk up to the bunker system.

A day and night in the 'j' had been a sharp learning curve.

INGLEBURN INFANTRY TRAINING CENTRE, EARLY 1967

A veteran who had served up at Bien Hoa with 1RAR told of the two Viet Cong teenagers who were ordered to carry two mortar bombs from Hanoi to Saigon along the Ho Chi Minh Trail. After being strafed, mortared and ambushed for three months, they dutifully delivered their arsenal to the South Vietnamese freedom fighters, who thanked them—and then asked them to go back and get another two. The vet laughed to himself over his beer, 'Fucking stupid Nogs.'

LUNCH AND HEARTBURN

Lang Phuoc Hai on Route 44 was a fishing village on the coast south-west of Nui Dat. This area of Phuoc Tuy province was low scrub, bamboo thickets and sand dunes rolling down to the South China Sea. The beaches were long, white and clean, with boats pulled up and fishing nets strung out to dry. The place told a story of peace in another time. During the battalion's Operation Atherton, 2RAR soldiers stripped off and plunged into the surf. As a reminder that this also was a war zone, a digger kicked an enemy mine and was killed, several others were wounded and casevaced by chopper.

Along this stretch of coast were gracious old French villas, the Vietnam Riviera, before the locals decided to kick the French out. Those villas were still there, although showing signs of war and neglect. Many were still occupied despite the bullet holes and shell shrapnel damage across the shining white walls.

Two days before the village search on Lang Phuoc Hai we had flown south from Nui Dat. It was a chance to orientate as to what was where in the south-west.

The first feature on the horizon was called the Horseshoe, an extinct volcano, the caldera making for an excellent permanent fire base position and observation point to the south, over-looking the town of Dat Do and the minefield fence.

The barbed wire fence that ran alongside Route 44 to the sea was constructed to stop the enemy moving from the east to the west. It was possibly the Task Force's greatest folly. The Australians had seeded the fence with 20 000 anti-personnel mines, and the VC had lifted 8000 or more to use against the allies. Those jam-can sized killers were now all over the province. The M16 mine, known as the 'jumping jack' or 'bouncing betty', was pressure-released and, after the foot was lifted, would shoot up into the air to groin height and explode. Needless to say where most of the shrapnel struck, and how much fear this put into any grunt who knew the jumping jacks were around.

South-west was a low mountain range, the Long Hais, which was circled by Route 44. The road swung back east along the coast to Lang Phuoc Hai. From the air you could look further west across low swamplands to the Cape St Jacques peninsula and the port of Vung Tau. Stretching further east from Lang Phuoc Hai was an area known as the Long Green, so-called because of its colouring on Army topographical maps. Low bush, bamboo, countless tracks and trails—Charlie's country, peppered with hides, tunnels and landmines.

Just a few months into 2RAR's tour and this area became one of the most loathed and feared operational zones in the province—due to the lives it had taken and the men it had maimed for very little return in way of enemy body count.

Trackers were deployed with other 2RAR and 7RAR units as part of the main group that would search Lang Phuoc Hai. While the Australian soldiers did the physical cordon and search, the local authorities, a mix of police and Army of the Republic of Vietnam (ARVN) along with Aussie civil affairs workers, would examine ID cards and collar ARVN draft dodgers. The search had to be done with 'discretion, caution and consideration'; in other words, don't kick the pigs or steal the chickens.

The enemy had been active down here. The ARVN had recently erected a sentry post outside the village on Route 44, a sandbagged bunker with a few coils of barbed wire. It had proved an irresistible attraction to the VC, who promptly pulverised the position with a round of rockets and satchel charges. So it fell to the Aussies—the military muscle in Phuoc Tuy—to move in and sort the mess out. In addition, it was only a month from local elections, and certainly Charlie would be active terrorising the population, hiding weapons and stashing food in little Lang Phuoc Hai.

It was late morning, and we were getting a taste of local village life. Blue and Simon were carrying the elderly and crippled from the huts and shacks as I sat down with Caesar to watch and pass comment. 'Ask her what she's doing tonight, Blue.'

'S'okay, mamasan. S'okay.' Blue held a fragile bundle of clothes and bones in his powerful arms, carrying the old woman out so her home could be searched by Ken and Thatch. Simon carried an old man, presumably the old woman's husband, piggyback style. He looked the real villain now that his mutton chops had spread down both sides of his face. Les was prodding rice bags with his bayonet and turning over bamboo mats like he was inspecting the specials on a clothing table.

Caesar had slumped for a doze in the shade, and I was leaning against a wall with my rifle in a position that made me look ready and alert, although I was thinking of some way I could brew up. It was during this time I became aware of a dog looking at me. Soldiers were milling around him, but the animal hadn't moved.

'What's the matter with you, boy?' I asked, and the dog began to move towards me. He was skinny, but hardly malnourished. What held me transfixed was the dog walked sideways, like a crab, not a normal trot over for a pat like the neighbourhood dog would have done.

'What's the matter with you, mate?' I edged closer, ignoring cautions the local fauna was riddled with disease, including rabies. He was now side on and looking straight ahead. I bent to pat him and then for some reason I pulled back. As I looked down, the dog turned his head and I realised I was looking straight into his exposed brain. Part of the side of the head that had been turned away from me was blown away, revealing a grey, wet mess.

I took two fast steps back and the dog continued to look at me with one good eye. Acidic phlegm was rising in my throat, and I grabbed Caesar's leash as he woke with a start. 'Come on, move. *Move!*'

Blue was suddenly in front of me as I part staggered down the street. 'You okay? You look like shit.'

I pointed back down the street. 'That dog's only got half a brain.' I put my hand over my mouth, certain I'd chuck.

Blue grinned, 'Yeah, so? You an' him should be good mates.'

Blue laughed and turned away, 'Jesus, I'm hungry. When the hell we gunna eat?'

I sat on the edge of a rice bund on the outskirts of the town and held Caesar close to me. For no reason I took out his brush and started to groom him, whispering 'You're a good dog, Caesar. Nothing's going to happen to you, mate.' I needed to reassure my dog, needed to reassure myself, there was a normality in this abnormal world where a dog walked about with only part of its head left, where everything was dangerous or damaged. I felt, for the first time in Vietnam, that I was isolated; there was a need to reach out, to hang onto something real.

There had been two continuous weeks of bush work, hopping from one rifle company to another. I hadn't seen Fergie for a fortnight. He was in the village search today, but with a group of trackers in another part of the hamlet. I looked back down the street which was a mixture of houses, many made from compressed Coke and beer cans and pieces of plastic that looked like US military-issue of some sort.

Alien. Everything was alien. The bend in the road was a threat, the ants were dangerous, every bug had a toxic bite. There were 130 species of snakes in this fucking place. Every square foot of dirt was potentially lethal. The words Thatch said after an all-night ambush in the rain came back to me: 'If it don't bite you, shoot you or blow you up, it'll shit on you.' During an ambush Thatch had sat in the rain under a clump of bamboo, and a flock of bantams that had made their home above the gunner's head shitted on him all night. His assistant on the machine-gun had lost patience before first light and attacked the fowls. It was just luck the terrorised birds didn't trigger the ambush.

There was often the question raised about whether the fauna in Vietnam had VC sympathies. JC had said to me earlier that morning: 'I've never seen looks of bloody hate like what's on these people's faces. They hate us. They don't want us here, they want the VC in here. Pete, I reckon the pigs in this place are bloody VC.'

I was still trying to pull myself together when a bunch of rifle company diggers walked up. We were standing talking on the road when the platoon commander approached.

'Take a lunch break and smoko. We'll move out in about half an hour.' He looked at me and the dog. 'Might as well stick with us. Move off the road into the paddi.'

I wandered into the dry paddi field with 10 or so other rifle company men, and we spread out in a rough defensive perimeter. I sat near a forward scout who was already opening a can of Vienna sausages. 'Hmm, not so bad,' he sniffed at the contents which were coated in a film of white slime and spooned them out with his bayonet. I had no stomach for food after the dog incident, and began to boil water while I had a smoke.

It was hot in the open paddi, and I got a good drink of

water into Caesar. Part way through the break there was a commotion on the road with what looked like an ARVN interpreter shouting at the platoon commander. The lieutenant left us and walked over while the local soldier kept shouting and pointing at us.

'What's up with the fucking Nog?' the scout spluttered, part way through his last sausage. 'Shut the fuck up. *'Didi mao!* Piss off, stupid!'

We were both distracted by the ruckus, and didn't notice when Caesar stood up and hunched down for a dump.

'Aw no, mate. No mate, *please.'*

The scout wasn't happy about a close crap spoiling his meal, which I thought reasonable and I unhooked the dog's leash and told him to move away. The dog padded off, still hunched, and 30 feet away started to defecate.

There was a shout from the road, the lieutenant had his hands cupped around his mouth. 'Everyone stay where you are. Do not move. You're having lunch in a minefield.'

My eyes locked with those of the forward scout. He began to stand. 'You're jokin'. No, you're *jokin'*!'

'Don't move. Sit down. Sit down!' I yelled at the man, at the same time swivelling around to look for the dog who was now sniffing at his pile of poo. A sensation I had never felt before washed down from my head to my boots. This was what they called freezing terror, I reckoned. It was paralysing, draining every smidgen of energy from your body in one horrific rush.

The scout looked at me, just managing to whisper, 'Can a dog set a mine off?' Then a calm came over me, training clicked in. I knew what to do and how to do it. I held my hand up, palm facing towards the dog. Tracking Wing,

Arthur Eather: *'There is no question obedience will be one of the most important parts of dog handling in Vietnam.'*

'Caesar!' He looked at me. 'Caesar, stay.' He froze looking at me. 'Caesar, sit!' I put my arm against my chest. He sat, looking straight at me. 'Caesar, down!' The dog extended his legs and slid onto his belly. 'Good dog. Caesar, stay!' Palm up and outwards again, and the dog responded with his tongue lolling out, eyes locked on me.

'Fuck. Fuck. Thank fuck for that,' the scout let out a whistle of air. He unsheathed his bayonet and began prodding around him. I slipped my hot coffee mug off my knife and started doing the same.

The calmness evaporated, and I was back into near panic; a helplessness that silently smothered you. Each square inch, every small disturbance in the baked earth of the stubbly paddi was now explosive. The scout had drawn his legs up under his chin and was sliding his knife in and out of the dirt, his lips were pulled back in a grimace and his tongue was clenched between his teeth. Other men sat like Buddhas, each involved in self-preservation with any sharp object at hand, gently prodding and probing.

I had cleared a small circle around myself and was now working out towards the dog.

Every so often I looked up from my haunched position and reassured the animal. 'Good, boy. Stay, *stay*.' I was aware with the sweat pouring down my own face that his black coat must have been cooking in the sun.

On the road, vehicles arrived, and there was shouting amid abuse and the crackle of radio transmissions.

I was dragging my webbing belt behind me while I crawled further out. I slumped and guzzled from my water bottle. Caesar saw me and started to rise. *'Down, sit. Down!*

Please, mate, it won't be long and I'll give you a drink.'

I was halfway to the dog when the sound of a chopper reached us. The Huey swung and dropped onto the road with a combat engineer mini-team who scrambled out with mine-clearing equipment. I felt a sudden panic again. *Would the dog go crackers at the chopper?* He didn't. The helicopter took off and swung out over the sea.

I was almost paralysed with the ache in my legs, trying to move in a half crawl and half crouch. The scout was quietly urging me on with encouragements: 'Careful, there might be one to your left, mate.'

'Just fucking shut up, *will ya*,' I yelled back at him.

The soldier looked at Caesar. 'He's a real obedient dog.'

My elbows were bleeding and I felt my neck seizing up as I tried to keep my head up while bent double, but it was amazing how the possibility of detonation and mutilation kept the mind focused.

There was a man next to me. I looked up. It was an engineer, sweeping a detector all around me.

'You're okay on the left. Roll over,' he said as he stepped past. 'That your dog up front?' The engineer smiled down at me.

I rolled on my back and looked up at the blue sky over Lang Phuoc Hai. 'Yeah. Thank Christ he does what he's bloody told.'

PHUOC TUY, FIRE SUPPORT BASE, 1968

'Hey, mate, your dog?'

The soldier was stripped to the waist and had emerged from the FSB's 105 gun area. Judging by his build he was an artilleryman. They were fitness mad, and lugging shells and pushing the artillery pieces around all day probably even developed muscles in their shit.

'Yeah, my dog.'

'Can I take him for a walk?'

I did a double take. Inside a fire base, just a few hundred yards or so in circumference, there wasn't space much to walk the dogs. Fergie and I managed to do a quick walk around in the morning so the animals could have a comfortable crap. Other than that they were tied to stakes all day, bored out of their skulls, while the handlers laid wire and filled sandbags or did sentry duty.

'Where do you want to take him?'

The gunner was stroking Caesar who was checking out the man's body smell.

'Show me mates at the guns. I love dogs. Had a kelpie in Armidale.'

I pricked up. 'You come from Armidale?'

'Yep.'

'You know how to cure acne?' The soldier gave me an odd look. 'Why, the dog got acne?'

'No, just an old joke. I can't let you take the dog, mate...unless you take his mate too. That might be okay.' I pointed at Marcus, panting under Fergie's hootchie.

'Yeah, right.'

'But you'll have to give them a real good walk, otherwise they sort of get upset they've been shortchanged, you know?'

'Yeah right.'

'That'll be outside the wire. Once round the perimeter will do it.'

'Yeah, okay. I'll get a mate and we'll do a run. Run sound okay?'

I feigned indecision. 'Yes, all right, make it a run. Do it every day once you've started though. They're like kids, once you start you can't just stop.'

The gunner was grinning all over his face. Taking the dogs leads, he jogged with Marcus and Caesar over to the gun pits.

Fergie came over, watching the artilleryman taking off with two tracking dogs. 'What did you do? Give them to the dropshorts?'

I gave him a punch on the arm. Three days later the dogs were still getting a walk in the morning and a good run at night.

BADLANDS

'Ever squeezed a woman's tit?'

You meet moronic people flying in choppers. Like the door-gunner called Scotty, who leaned over and asked the question.

'Goes like this,' he said. High over Phuoc Tuy, Scotty leaned into space and held an open hand into the wind blast, then opened and closed his fingers. He indicated to me to try it. I slid over to the door and held my palm out. When I opened and closed my hand there was a feeling similar to squeezing soft flesh. Door-gunners were renowned for their small minds, I told Scotty, who only grinned broadly and asked me if my dog was 'still fucking stupid around choppers'.

He'd seen Caesar's antics before, and laughed again when the dog went ballistic landing at Eagle Farm. I hitched a ride from the chopper pad down to Support Company. It had been raining, and everything was red mud. I put Caesar in his kennel, and noticed that Marcus was gone. Bob and Bill were in their tent, and I heard the sounds of Armed Forces Radio and the song they had been flogging to death in the past month, Bobby Vinton and *Lonely Soldier*. Back in my tent, Les stuck his head in and said Fergie and Marcus were out with Bravo Company. As an afterthought he added, 'Did you hear that Cassius was dead?'

I went dumb for a moment. Norm's dog, Cassius, over at 7RAR was *dead*?

'Died of heat exhaustion is all we've heard. Shit of a thing. What happened to you on the search—some strife?'

My head was still spinning. I hadn't seen Norm but for

a brief visit to the 7RAR Tracking Team lines after arriving in country. I sat down on my cot.

'Yeah, we had lunch in a minefield yesterday. It was something different.'

I started to strip off my filthy greens. I stank like hell, and wondered if it was coming from the painful sores that were ulcerating around my hips where the webbing belt was still chaffing. I reminded myself to get to the Regimental Aid Post before the infection got any worse. Everything in Vietnam went septic within days.

I had my towel around my waist and a block of soap in my hand when Les came running back. 'Scramble! We're off out again.'

Bob already was out of his tent and yelling at me. 'D Company contact. Fast as you can, mate!'

I went into autopilot, dropped the towel, pulled on fresh greens and hauled my pack up onto my back. I was down on rations I'd eaten in the past two days, but I could fill up the water bottles pretty quickly on the way to the kennels. By the time I had Caesar out, the Land Rover was pulling up at the Support Company and we were on our way to the chopper pad with the dog hanging out of the vehicle, sucking up the wind.

In a minute the Huey was down, we were on the floor, and there was the familiar shudder as the pilot gunned his machine and we were out over the rubber heading south west. I was back on Scotty's aircraft, and he gave me the thumbs up and shouted, 'I bet you didn't even have time to piss'. He jabbed a finger out to the horizon and the coast. 'Heavy contact, Long Green.'

The rifle platoon had that look of contact all over it—eyes wide, hunched into fire positions; silence, anticipation, what next? A sandy foot track wound out among clumps of bamboo and in front of us was a pool of blood. There had been a full-on engagement and the VC had bugged out, but not before getting a full belt of M60 from the forward section gunner. They had returned fire and there were cartridge cases everywhere to prove it.

The forward scout approached, speaking in a hoarse voice. 'They've got AKs, and they are ready for a fucking blue. Just watch yourself.' He spoke without looking at me. He was still jumping out of his skin with the adrenaline rush that comes in a firefight.

Les was covering me while I harnessed up, and I looked behind him but couldn't see any other trackers through the thick bush. There was something not right; we usually had some sort of conflab before we got going. Les looked at me and whispered 'They said, "Go".'

'What?'

'They said to start tracking.'

With some reluctance I shook out the lead. We had landed in a clearing which was surrounded by armoured personnel carriers. The APCs had been rushed up from the Lang Phuoc Hai search area after the contact because there was every indication the enemy was going to stay to fight this one out. He saw the Long Green as his territory, he knew this piece of ground and was obviously staying around. This indicated we were near a camp or bunker system. D Company also had said it was sure the Viet Cong contacted were an advance party for a far larger group. All well-armed.

None of this made me feel any better as Caesar stopped for a short squirt on a bush. 'Easy boy, easy. Seek 'em. *Get 'em!*'

I pulled the Armalite up into firing position with one hand and balanced it on my basic pouch, noticing the foot track was wide and an increasing number of footprints were evident. It registered that they were combat boots, not Ho Chi Minh sandals. There was blood all the way.

Caesar's head went up and down, air scenting and picking up powerful smell on the ground. The bush got thicker and higher, but the track was widening. I slowed down to allow the follow-up troops to catch up. I knew basic infantry tactics dictated you never walked on a trail, so the platoon would have been working its way through the scrub both sides of the track. *They're damned good,* I thought, *can't hear a sound. Just hope they're keeping up when this little duck hits the shit.*

I felt my mouth starting to dry out and I turned to see how Les was going. He wasn't far behind, rifle up, eyes scanning left and right. I turned back to find I'd suddenly reached a T-junction. We'd done about a click on the map. Caesar stopped in the middle of the junction. I panicked and urged him on. The T-section would provide at least a two-way fire lane if Charlie was waiting. But Caesar was looking straight at the clump of bamboo at the head of the junction. He didn't point, he dropped his head and flattened his ears.

'Heaven's sake, Caesar. Move your ass,' I hissed.

He dropped his head to the ground, started back like he had been hit in the face, then turned and walked back to me. He then sat directly on top of my foot. What the hell was he doing? *Arthur Eather, Bulli Pass: Don't just plough on, it could be a punji pit or a mine.*

He suddenly started pushing at my leg. I had never seen anything like this before. He was insistent. I bent down, hearing movement in the scrub alongside as the platoon moved closer.

'For shit's sake, dog...'

Like a flash from a camera, the trees all around us lit up for a millisecond. The detonation was like a sledgehammer in my back and I went up and forward, slamming down face first into the sand. My rifle speared into the ground, barrel first, and it felt like my eardrums had been blown in. A searing pain burned down my back and I felt hot liquid squirt down my legs.

'Jesus, I'm hit!' I shoved my hand down the front of my pants, praying I hadn't got *the* wound. Relief, I had only pissed myself. At that moment it started to rain leaves and small branches.

Simultaneously I heard the scream *'Mines, mines*. Don't move!' I lifted my head to see the war dog staring straight into my eyes with that fine-mess-you've-got-us-into-this-time look. I fought to clear my head and get my thoughts straight. Go into standard contact drill: what had we hit? A ground mine, or was it command detonated? Would the VC counterattack now? Who had been hit? How many wounded? Shit, how many dead?

I twisted round to see Les lying face down holding his hat on his head with his hand. 'Les! *Les!* What the hell's going on? Who's hit?'

The coverman shouted out to someone behind him while I spun around to peer up and down the junction. I was so exposed I felt sick, and edged back into a bush, pulling Caesar with me, holding him tight between my legs. It was next to useless, but cover from view was better than no cover at all.

Les was calling up to me, 'Platoon commander's gone, signaller's gone and…maybe three others. We're smack in the middle of a minefield. How are you?'

'Apart from standing out like a shithouse in a sand dune, I'm all right.'

'All right? God, who was I kidding? I'd just led the whole

platoon into a minefield.' I thanked God I hadn't seen what happened behind me. The diggers had been in the bush on both sides of the track—standard practice, you never, ever walk on a used trail. It was tough, slow, you were scratched to hell, but you weren't about to be ambushed...or step on a mine. That's what the enemy had done; laid mines both sides of the trail, and then run down the middle of the track. Charlie knew Aussie tactics by now...and had sucked us right into it.

There was talking now, and I thought I heard a moan and groan then the static of radio and whispered urgent instructions over the net. Les was sitting up, looking at me. He shrugged when I asked him what was happening. He asked the soldier behind him, then turned back. 'Dustoff... incoming...they're securing the area.' I looked down the T-junction. Clear.

I felt incredibly thirsty, and eased a water bottle out of its pouch. Empty. I tried another. Barely a mouthful. I had forgotten to fill them up. I scrabbled through my pack and found one half full. I trickled the water into a mug and shoved it under Caesar's nose. It was gone in a gulp.

Caesar suddenly sat up and his ears shot out. I went into a fire position. The whine and thud grew louder. Choppers! I slapped the dog on the head, then hugged him. 'You bloody idiot.'

The dustoff was overhead and a litter was already on its way down when the second chopper came thundering in. It tilted and I saw the door-gunner swing his '60s up, scanning for VC. The Huey had a combat engineer team on board, and it circled while the wounded were winched up into the other Casevac helicopter. I counted three Stokes litters.

Now there was the sound of APCs growling close by.

They were chopping through the bush towards us, and I winced: *great, they'll hit another mine and shower us with shrapnel.* No sooner had the thought occurred than I heard a bang and saw black smoke shoot upwards. Then another bang.

'For Chrissake, don't let 'em come down here,' shouted Les to no-one in particular.

The engines cut and there was silence again. I was going giddy with thirst. I pushed Caesar as far as I could into the shade of the scrub. Two engineers appeared pushing past Les, sweeping left to right. A machine-gunner was next to them. They reached me.

'Stay there mate,' one swept around me, adjusting his earphones. He looked into the bush at the dog. 'G'day, mate. Didn't I see you the day before yesterday at the village?'

'You got any water? Water, any water?' I could hardly speak.

Les was already next to me and dropped a water bottle in my lap, filling a mug at the same time for Caesar. The two engineers were at the junction and kneeling down, speaking quietly. One turned to me. 'You come up this far?'

'No, the dog did, up to the bamboo.'

For a few minutes the two men worked quietly on their knees and pushed sand around. I wasn't interested. One of the sappers came back to me. 'There's two M16 jumpin' jacks on the track ahead, and they're wired with detonator cord to an unexploded bomb. Could be a naval shell or 500lb from an air strike. Enough anyway to take the whole platoon out, take the company out, although it was meant for an APC. The carrier hits the M16, blows the main bomb charge—no more carrier. Simple as a fuck. The dog's your salvation. Good job you didn't go walkeys up there, mate. *Really* fucking lucky.'

Les reached in to touch Caesar's nose. 'Thank sweet Jesus for you, you freaky little fucker.'

I struggled to remember where I'd heard that phrase before. Yeah, the big black basketballer who'd welcomed us to Vietnam.

We moved quietly back to the clearing and the APCs. Two of them had track repairs to look forward to for the rest of the night after running over anti-personnel mines.

No one was saying much; only basic instructions and debriefing, all spoken in hushed tones. The platoon commander had lost both legs, the signaller was critical, two others were serious and there were shrapnel wounds to other soldiers. The jumping jack had caught a group of men close together, shredding them with lethal fragments of red-hot metal. For a moment I sat and went through life's what-ifs. What if I had pushed the dog, trod on the M16 in the junction and detonated the massive main charge? I'd be dead at 19 years of age, there'd be a crater in the Long Green and most of Delta Company would be distributed in bits and pieces around the God-forsaken place.

I expected abuse or at the very least dark looks. There was none from the diggers of Delta. I even got a 'Well done, mate,' which was hardly the right compliment for the worst day in our lives. I lit up a nerve-calming smoke while a few other blokes rubbed the dog's ears.

He didn't deserve to be in this bloody hole. We were asked to come here, or were sent here. A mongrel dog with a stuffed ear should be running around the streets or in a paddock playing up, biting the postie, getting into a fight, chewing a bone on the back lawn, even sniffing some bitch's arse. I pulled out a brush and started to groom him. We sat on the edge of the clearing until he gave a low growl. A digger looked at me and reached for his rifle. 'What's the matter with him?'

'Chopper's coming.'

The soldier looked around the sky. 'I can't hear any choppers.'

'He can.'

SOUTHERN PHUOC TUY PROVINCE, 1967

South-west of Nui Dat, Fergie was on the track of an enemy group. He had unknowingly tracked into a minefield. He was yards from death or mutilation when the alert platoon sergeant noticed a skull-and-cross-bones nailed to a tree with MINE written on it in small red letters. Who put the mines in was unclear. That was the trouble with Vietnam, no-one took responsibility for anything.

The senior NCO's instructions were brief and clear—he told his men to walk backwards 100 yards; retreat they way they had come. The sergeant didn't figure a dog couldn't walk too well backwards. Fergie picked up 60 pounds of labrador and struggled in reverse gear the full 100 yards. I told him I didn't think anyone anywhere had ever accomplished such a feat, certainly not with the threat of being blown to bits as an added handicap.

Fergie shook his head and thought for a minute. 'I admit I was shagged. Next time he can find his own way out. God those bloody dogs weigh a bit.'

CRIME AND PUNISHMENT

The Huey tilted and slowly moved forward over the Delta position. Looking down there were just a few APCs now, crawling through the bush like fat, grey slugs while here and there soldiers were making their way back out on patrol. The war goes on. The Long Green faded, the tracks and trails became a spider web again as the chopper gained height and turned towards Nui Dat.

I couldn't shake the feeling of blame and loss. My jaws ached with the teeth-clenching tension from the past hours, and my back was killing me. I wondered for a moment if there really may have been shrapnel buried in there. I'd heard the stuff could be the size of match heads and kill you by simply penetrating the ear canal or punching its way up your nostril, straight through to the brain. Dead, and not a mark on you.

Caesar was asleep on the floor when we touched down. Rain again and this time no lift. I walked back to the kennels, grateful there was no-one I had to talk to. I shoved the dog in his run and he bounded up and down with Marcus. *Have a nice day, old dog? Yeah, my stupid handler walked us into a bloody minefield. How about yourself?*

Down through the rubber, across the road and into Tracking Wing's lines, looking at the ground the whole way. I felt like shit, and definitely would have looked like shit. Fergie was writing a letter, sitting at the table with his shirt off, and Ken was lying on his cot, arm over his face, snoring. I sat on my stretcher and eased out of the webbing.

'How'd it go Pete? Want a brew?'

I sipped at the hot coffee, and noticed I was starting to

shake. 'Hit a minefield and got cut up real bad down the fucking Long Green.'

Fergie grunted. 'The best thing for that place is a full on B-52 strike all day for a week.'

'Oh, yeah? As long as all the bombs go *off*. They're using our own unexploded stuff to blow us up. Fucking Nogs.'

There was silence. I picked up my rifle, it was clogged and covered in sand. I removed the magazine and broke the weapon, stock from butt. Bolt out and wipe away the dirt. Pull through into the barrel, then a general clean up with an old shaving brush. Light oil. Reassemble the two parts, bolt back in. Close the weapon, pull back the bolt, lock. Magazine on.

I felt tears coming up into my eyes. I was having some sort of reaction. Shaking again, I heard the groans…felt myself sliding sideways and tried to pull myself together…hit the bolt release and it slammed forward, carrying a round into the chamber. I fired the action.

For months the Colt AR-15 had been part of my life, an old friend. I had stripped and cleaned it scores of times. In the bush, in the dark. The infantryman's relationship with his weapon was almost intimate; clichéd but absolute truth. The Armalite fired on semi and fully automatic with a muzzle velocity of 3200 feet per second; 700 rounds a minute if you kept the trigger back. The 5.56mm round was tiny by any measure, a .223 calibre. But its hitting power was shattering. I knew, I had looked down at the result of a burst of rounds from the 'toy, plastic rifle'.

The moment I fired the action I knew I'd got it wrong. I had put the magazine on *before* I released the bolt, instead of after. The round was now chambered and the firing pin struck home. The explosion in the small tent was deafening as the weapon fired and the ejected shell case pinged across the floor. Ken and Fergie hit the duckboards simultaneously, and in that cold-as-death moment I realised I had shot my dog handler mate. Fergie was flat on his stomach, lying in a pool of spreading liquid. He turned his head to look up at me. '*Jesus*, Peter. Are you all right?'

There was an instant of relief and I stared speechless at the Armalite lying across my legs. The bullet had passed by Fergie's neck and punched a clean, pencil-sized hole in the tent flap. The liquid was coffee on the floor. He jumped up, grabbed the rifle from me and made it safe.

'You've AD'd Peter. Gonna run for it?' Ken was telling me in one sentence I had committed the worst of no-nos: an accidental discharge, and I was in Deep Serious, would certainly face a charge—an A4 in military terms—that would carry a heavy penalty. Ken was suggesting I run. Funny. Where do you run to in the middle of Vietnam?

In less than a minute two Regimental Police were in the tent taking my name, rank and number. It had been a day to long remember and I was finding if the war didn't kill you, it could still take you apart inch by suffering inch.

Regular morning routine, Nui Dat...Out of bed at 6am and a short walk from the tent to the road outside Support Company orderly room. Line up, yawn, scratch while the daily Paludrine pill is handed out. This small, white tablet is a compulsory medication to prevent malaria, and you swallow it quickly. Really quickly. If it dwelt in the mouth for more than a second the revolting taste would almost induce vomiting.

After the pill, a shave outside the tent while Armed Forces Vietnam Radio hammered out Aretha Franklin's *R-E-S-P-E-C-T* for the first of a dozen plays it would get that day. Next, Otis Redding's *Dock Of The Bay*, then the news and a round-up of the war, province by province

'...after heavy fighting around Dak To, allied forces casualties have been described as light.' Back to the music and requests 'from the light fire team at Long Binh to all the guys at the 183rd, here's Billy Joe Royal's *Down in the Boondocks*.' AFVN Radio was soul music at certain times of the day, and as far as the Australians were concerned a lot of it may as well have been beamed in from another galaxy. Between the 'fantastic black plastic' there was Adrian Cronauer and cautions to 'keep your '16 clean' and 'get a free education when you get home', courtesy of the GI Bill.

Into boots and shorts and a walk from the tent to the cookhouse, where there was yellow sloppy powdered egg, a scoop of beans in ham sauce and two rashers of bacon. This all went together on a US Forces-style multi-compartmented personal stainless-steel tray which you carried the short distance to the mess hall. Here two milk urns had been placed in the middle of the floor, one containing sickly sweet chocolate-flavoured milk. Plenty of tea or coffee, and two or three cigarettes before washing the tray in a cut-down 44-gallon drum of hot, soapy water, then back to the lines. Equipment check, ammunition check, personal weapon stripped and cleaned. Dirty greens were bundled off base for washing by the Vietnamese, and the medic might drop round to do a foot inspection. By now men were in various stages of footrot, chronic Asian tinea, angry heat rashes to the back and front of the body, and anyone who ever suffered acne was getting a real dose by now.

While some pottered, others began the interminable task of raking up dead leaves, or were allocated duties from dixie bashing in the mess halls to chain-sawing dead rubber trees. Fergie and I took the dogs for a walk and did morning obedience, then it was a last run for the dogs before they were fed. We never got tired of watching the dogs play. It was an anchor of normal in a world of abnormal. Caesar and Marcus were true buddies; chase and roll was their favourite leisure activity outside of sleeping. Marcus would wind up to a fast gallop, while Caesar pursued the big labrador and tried to bring him down with a barrel roll. Caesar would then take flight, with Marcus at his heels striving for a canine-style ankle tap. Both dogs would eventually collapse in a pile, bodies heaving like billows.

Marcus was the mobile garbage disposal unit who could pick up a whiff of sizzling sausages half a click away. Like many labs, he was a born scavenger, dedicating his life to ratting out food scraps or separating Fergie from the last of his spaghetti and meatballs. Droopy-eyed and languid, Marcus exploded when he hit a scent trail and hammered at it until exhausted. Like the late Cassius, there was always the worry with Marcus he would crash and burn from fatal heat exhaustion.

Caesar was less intense, he trotted around the trees at Nui Dat, spending minutes concentrating on one single smell. He was an inveterate back-roller; at any given time he would drop and roll on his back. I suspected he was picking up animal smell to disguise his own, a trait typical of field dogs. He didn't scavenge for food, but picked up his bowl in his mouth and was often standing alert at tucker time before we reached the kennels with their fresh meat.

I pulled two weeks field punishment and a $40 fine for the accidental discharge. The money didn't hurt, but the field punishment was something to get into a sweat about. It was the equivalent of striped pyjamas, a sledgehammer and break-ing rocks in the hot sun. Possibly a lot harder.

I was put under the control of the battalion's Regimental Police. I would work from first light until dusk. I would be allowed to look after my war dog 'in respect to whatever was deemed necessary for his care and wellbeing' for an hour in the morning and at night. The remainder of the day I would carry out hard labour duties within the unit, and out of hours fill sandbags wearing full field kit and helmet.

I saddled up and made my way down to the RPs' tent. I was fuming at the commanding officer, Lieutenant-Colonel Noel 'Chick' Charlesworth. He was respected and admired by all his men, but as soon as I swung my pack on I felt that urge to rip the bastard's throat out. He asked how it happened. I told him I'd had a bad day, being blown up and being a bit out of sorts by the time I got back to the lines. The CO sat with his hands as if in prayer, and it was hard to tell whether he was looking at me or watching a lizard on the closest rubber tree through his dark glasses. After sentencing he said that I 'must learn to be more careful'. The sort of comment grandads make to errant children who trip over the cat.

The RP sergeant was waiting for me and took me up near the dog kennels. There was a Mount Everest of sand and a single shovel alongside three piles of new sandbags. The RP watched while I hammered three steel stakes into the ground to support the empty bag and I hooked the first one on. Only about a thousand to go.

'Where am I supposed to stack them?' I queried after the first one was filled and tied off.

He turned and pointed to Caesar and Marcus who were watching me from the runs. 'You're sandbagging the kennels.'

I swear he was grinning all over his face when he saw the expression on mine. But he had turned and gone with the parting remark: 'I'll be checking on you, private. Don't slack off.'

I'd spent all day washing out lavatory blocks; Blow Fly duty. Nui Dat toilets were corrugated iron sheds with mosquito netting around the top, a concrete floor and five thunderboxes. A deep pit beneath the slab took the waste. A few months, depending on use, and it was filled and the process repeated elsewhere.

After tea I donned full gear again and started filling bags. Each shovelful was murder as I had to bend and take the full weight of the pack onto my neck. I piled the bags into a wheelbarrow and unloaded them next to the kennels. Marcus and Caesar sat mute, watching me. *What the hell is he doing, old dog?*

Dunno, but very nice of him. Sorry about the bad luck, boss. But good of you to make life safer for us guys.

I felt sure by the time it got dark I'd be given the word to break until morning. The RP appeared with a hurricane lamp just before last light and informed me I had to make up the time I spent looking after the dog. He lit the lamp and said he'd be back.

I kept filling, placed the lamp on top of the barrow and pushed and strained along what was by now a well-worn track to the kennels. Marcus had given up watching the show and retired to his bedboard. Caesar stayed up, lying with his head up against the arcmesh watching me with obvious approval as his blast wall got higher.

By the time week one was up I was the most buggered I'd felt in my life. All day doing lavatories and cleaning out grease traps, and at night, sandbagging. I took the jibes good-naturedly: 'How's the lady with the lamp doing?' Fergie and other trackers kept up a steady stream of cold VB in the corner of Caesar's kennel for a night-time guzzle.

Cleaning the toilet blocks was demeaning, but kneeling in

front of the grease trap near the kitchen was worse. The stink and glop, that looked like semen, was actually absorbed into the skin, and Ken and Fergie were giving me The Look.

By week two I was physically devastated. A look in the mirror during shaving showed a thin, callow youth, skin yellowing, resembling a victim from a death camp. I was praying for the war to start again.

Caesar never went to bed while I was building the wall, which by now was almost completely around the kennel block. After they had been fed, Fergie walked them both while I grabbed an hour on the bed, in a state of total exhaustion.

After his walk Caesar lay in his run, watching me. I occasionally slumped on the bags and he pushed his nose through the fence with an encouraging lick. Fergie, Ken and Simon kept the beers in the kennel corner.

Like every digger, I counted days left to the end of the tour. Now I was counting minutes and hours to the end of this hell. It finally came, and the RP told me tomorrow I'd do the lavatory blocks and he wanted another hour's work that night; then 14 days field punishment was over.

Next morning I swear I saw both dogs making the sand-bagged walls their own by pissing on them.

HAT DICH AREA, NORTH-WEST PHUOC TUY, JANUARY 1968 – PART 1

It was like a used-car lot for armoured personnel carriers. This was the 3/5 Cavalry, a US unit with a long tradition. In another time they rode down hard on the Indians. In 1968 they were chasing the enemy at full stick, 11 tons propelled by diesel and petrol V8 motors. The detachment may have swapped their horses for horsepower, but still stuck to tradition and had circled the APCs to form a stockade. The impression created was that of a used-car yard. All that was missing were the price tags on each tank.

The Cavalry sergeant who greeted us carried a steel helmet in one hand and a pistol in the other. 'You the Aussie doggie people? Good, we've been getting our ass shot off.'

There was no sitting around or taking a smoke. In minutes the sergeant had hustled up six men as a chase party and was striding over towards the thick bush, talking to Bob at the top of his voice. He had the most booming, penetrating voice I'd ever heard. Ho Chi Mnh would have been sitting up listening in Hanoi.

'Gooks came up here, fired like fuck and bugged out. Took two of my men out. I'd really like you to find these people.'

I half expected Bob to say 'Yes sir!' and salute. He just nodded at me and pointed at the ground. 'Get him going here, mate.'

Caesar hit the scent trail running and bee-lined for the thicker jungle. The American sergeant was still shouting at his men as we slipped under the canopy. 'Keep your shit wired up tight and keep the goddamn noise down!'

After 10 minutes Caesar pointed, and straight ahead I picked up rows of enemy weapon pits stretching to my left and right. Beyond them, even in the poor light, I could see tier after tier of bunkers. In the dead silence of the shadows there was no movement. I gaped for a moment. God, this was fucking huge.

I croaked at Bob. 'Bunkers, huge complex. Back up, back up. Quick.'

FAST TRACKING

The next big operation was launched in a cloud of dust, diesel, heat and humidity. At Luscombe Field the American choppers droned in and picked up 7RAR, while most of the 2RAR rifle companies were ferried out in APCs. Our destination was an area code-named the May Tao Secret Zone in the north-east of Phuoc Tuy. The search-and-destroy mission was to target a region where the VC and NVA had built a staging base for food production and communications; a large logistic network of camps and trails had been established in heavy to moderate forest. The allied operation included Vietnamese and American Forces, the 3/5 Cavalry.

The Tracking Team and Anti-Tank Platoon were initially tasked with the protection of one of the fire support patrol bases (FSPBs), where the big 105 howitzers and a detach-ment of armoured personnel carriers were being dug in. These bases, as big as football ovals, were ringed with wire, sandbagged bunkers and weapon pits—like foxholes in another war. The fire base would support the rifle companies now being dropped into jungle locations across the May Tao Secret Zone. As the companies patrolled, the guns were able to track and lay support if contact with the enemy occurred.

Quite often the FSPB was literally chopped out of the jungle. Before the guns were airlifted from the 'Dat, infantry cleared the forest of enemy and secured the sector, while engineers dropped trees, levelled the ground and raised earth bunds. That was according to the textbook. In typical Army fashion things never went to plan, and the guns were flown in and wire hastily thrown up around the perimeter, while it was every man for himself to get below ground before nightfall.

This raised serious risks: it was a recurring and chaotic situation, and very often the enemy was arriving in numbers before the troops had adequate defences up. Good tactics on the part of Charlie. The fire bases became like a magnet to the enemy, who would strike hard and fast at an unprepared force, with the prime objective of neutralising the 105s.

With this foremost in our minds, we had our shovels out and were hacking away at the hard earth while wire was being strung out around the base. I tied Caesar up to a steel picket, and was down a good 12 inches creating what was called a shell scrape by the time the Chinooks began arriving with the 105s slung beneath them. Fatigue was forgotten during the furious pace of 'digging in'. Secrecy in planning was all very well, but neon signs couldn't have advertised a major op was up and running better than the air traffic.

I dug alongside Ken. We were paired up on the perimeter, and it was about 50 feet to the next pair, Simon and Fergie, then around to Thatch and Twiggy on the machine-gun. Pits were also sunk in depth around the base, so if the outer ring was breached in an attack the VC would still have a second wall of fire to break through. We didn't dwell on an attack that size, but concentrated on shifting enough dirt to get our body below ground level in the event of a rocket or mortar attack. I worked hard, extending my pit so the dog would also fit in.

Night fell, we stood to and waited for an assault. Nothing came but the usual blackness, and I was rostered on the M60 for an hour shift. I took Caesar with me and followed the nylon cord around to Thatch snoring at the gun pit, where we huddled down and stared out at the tree line. It was a dark but not totally black night—there was some reflected light because of the clear sky. We had starlight scopes on the fire base, which you could use if you thought you saw movement on the tree-line. The scope gave a green, unreal floating sensation when you looked through it. A flare, or even a striking match, returned a brilliant flash in the view-finder. Caesar didn't sleep while I was awake on sentry; he waited until we got back to our own hole, where I rolled in the camouflage silk before he put his head down between his paws. I only found out after arriving in Vietnam that I had a war dog who snored like a bloody trooper.

The weather had been out of kilter during our tour, but as soon as we were out of Nui Dat the monsoon came cruising by. The afternoon rain fell in curtains and it was so intense it hurt when it hit exposed skin. Weapon pits filled and men staggered around the fire base like drunks. Red mud stuck to everything—caked webbing and equipment, and ate its way into the pores of the skin. Jungle greens became saturated and covered in a veneer of red, then turned as hard as cardboard when the sun broke through. For the next two days misery prevailed.

Contacts started coming in. Bravo and Charlie Company: bunkers. Delta and Alpha: ambush. Further north the 3/5 Cavalry had bumped major VC/NVA. Casualties were described in regulation fashion as 'light'. The guns at the fire base went into overdrive, and the ground rippled under the concussion, or shock wave. The dog got a case of the shakes, and for a few minutes there was unreal silence while the eardrums de-popped. I was thinking of a hot chocolate drink when Bob called out, 'Saddle up. We're moving.'

I hoisted my pack and was hit with a flash thought: something made me ensure the winch jacket was strapped to the top of the pack mainframe. The Huey came floating in, and we were on board just as another downpour hit. A rifle platoon had triggered a contact in thick jungle west of the

FSPB. The door-gunner shouted: 'Two VC are KIA and one digger is WIA. Other VC have made off. I hear plenty of blood.'

Problem: the contact had occurred under thick canopy. I breathed a sigh of relief I had the winch coat ready for Caesar. In minutes we were over the location with rain streaming across the helicopter windows and blowing into the passenger bay. I clutched Caesar's collar while Bob and Simon took turns swinging out on the winch arm and in a moment both men were gone into the trees. The pilot looked at me with an urgent hurry-up expression on his face. I didn't blame him—this was a hot zone, and any moment he could cop a burst of AK fire. A 'sitting fuck' was what Scotty called a hovering chopper.

I had the winch jacket on Caesar, who was giving me anxious looks until the door-gunner grabbed him and hooked onto the D-ring. The dog was gone, and by the time I readied myself and my equipment, the winch hook was back up. I squeezed my eyes shut as soon as I swung out. The thrashing rotors, the wash of wind and rain and the prospect of a bullet between the legs made me curse the day I volunteered for Trackers. I hit one tree and rebounded onto another. I twisted to look up at the Iroquois rocking in the wind. *What the hell am I doing here?* Another thump and bump, and I was on the deck. I grabbed Caesar from Simon, who cleared my winch line and waved the helicopter away. Next, winch harness off, the dog and tracking harness at the ready.

Bob had been briefed. We examined the two dead VC and then checked the blood on the trail. It seemed the enemy had waited in ambush and fired on the scout. The platoon had gone into full contact drill and fought its way out. I shook the lead loose and Simon took up cover position, M79 grenade launcher over his shoulder and SLR rifle at the ready.

We plunged straight into the wet and gloom, and Caesar had his nose down for 500 yards until we reached a clearing in the jungle. The dog pointed. I went to one knee and saw nothing at first, then, in an almost comical manner, I spotted a black hat bobbing along through the shoulder-high grass. It looked like a man out for a walk after a noon rainshower; unconcerned, indifferent to the fact a dozen men were ready to kill him. All that was missing with him was an umbrella.

'VC,' I hissed at Simon who moved up quickly. 'Bloody hell,' he whispered, ''tis too!'

He unslung his M79 and pulled a HE grenade round from his bandolier. It was like an oversized shotgun cartridge with a swollen explosive head. The M79 broke like a shotgun, and the round slipped in. It was fired from the shoulder or the waist, and gave a distinct 'dupe' sound; the US forces called their grenadiers 'dupers'. The 40mm bomb slammed down in the middle of the clearing with a crump, and without hesitation Simon had popped off another round. Anyone within five yards of the explosion would be killed by shrapnel. 'I reckoned that cleaned his sinuses out,' Simon grinned at me. I yelled back, '*Contact!*'

The coverman had been clever using his grenade launcher in the high grass; much better than an indiscriminate blast of small-arms fire. The rifle section extended line to our right flank, and Bob yelled to Simon to cease firing while the first section swept across the clearing.

'Jesus, that was short and sharp.' I was panting, not from exertion as much as the sudden rush of action.

The platoon took over and encircled the clearing. One VC was found KIA, but it was likely that had been from the main ambush contact, not Simon's bombs. Bob did a visual search and found no further sign, and the track was considered lost. Nightfall was less than an hour off and we prepared for a wet night with the rifle platoon.

I sat again in the dark and, much to my surprise, found myself praying. I hadn't said prayers since I was a kid. I finished mumbling for Jesus to keep me safe. I looked down at my filthy boots with the leash wrapped around my ankle. 'And God bless my dog.'

HAT DICH AREA, NORTH-WEST PHUOC TUY, JANUARY 1968 – PART 2

I followed Bob while he worked his way back through the undergrowth to tell the Americans there was a massive bunker system only hundreds of yards from their APC stockade.

'Bunkers, huh? Right I'll bring some heavy stuff in.' The sergeant walked away talking into the radio at full blast. We were switching looks between each other. Maybe we should give the guy a megaphone so he could tell every major NVA division in South Vietnam we were right here. Next second a shot rang out and we dived for cover.

'Hello? Can you hear that? Wait.'

Another shot, and the sergeant appeared holding his pistol aloft. Bang. 'Can you hear that?'

The big American looked at us lying there, puzzlement all over his face. 'You guys okay? No gooks here. We gotta go, big shits coming.'

Bob looked at me and Thatch and whispered: 'Let's go. Fast, out.'

The first salvo came in and huge fountains of earth shot up through the trees. True to his word the Yank had brought 'heavy shit' in. Over the explosions behind us he was still shouting while we made our way back. 'I find using a shot or two over the radio gets things done a lot quicker. Brings home to those on the guns we are under attack and need some big shit fast.'

I patted Caesar on the way back. Every day in this country introduced you to some new madness.

TRAVELLIN' NORTH

November 4 dawned. Watery sky. Darkness in the tree line, retreating shadows, and the last moments of silence before we stood down to begin morning routine. I looked up to see Corporal Bill approaching in a big hurry, worry all over his face. This was urgent for sure because he didn't have his clipboard under his arm.

I had always liked Bill. He was quiet, almost introspective. Stuck to regulations, but ignored petty indiscretions of Army life; if you were drunk he'd tell you to go to bed without an argument. Others would A4 you. Bill also had a connection with the younger soldiers like myself that was almost paternal. He was a career soldier in his late thirties, a family man who had done Malaya and Borneo and, unlike other soldiers who had served there, didn't come on with the 'our jungle was thicker than your jungle'. Bill was predictable, reliable and not easily fazed. Just the sort of wheel you needed in charge in Vietnam. With this bloke you'd likely stay alive.

'No duties on the wire today, mate. We're going up to the Yanks, the 3/5 Cavalry. They've requested Trackers. You and the dog, okay?' Bill had his rifle resting across his basic pouch, his sleeves already rolled down, and seemed ill at ease. He had that look of being asked to do something either distasteful or dangerous. Not a good sign. If Bill could detour around an undesirable chore, he would do it with great evasive skill. That was another thing I liked about him. In this case, whatever it was, he was landed with it. I asked him if he meant we were going to track with the Yanks.

'They've been land clearing and have been hit about half a dozen times—rockets, a few KIA on both sides, and they

want to try a follow-up, so they're sending a chopper for us.'
Bill wheeled and went back to his pit. I trotted over to
Fergie and told him he was now on standby.

Bob and Bill stood with me outside the wire waiting for
the helicopter for a good half-hour before Caesar pricked
up. The drone became a dull throb then a deafening clatter
as the chopper wheeled over the fire base and landed almost
on top of us. Caesar went more berserk than usual, then
plunged forward. He was airborne as he hit the inside deck
of the aircraft, skated over the floor and went flying through
the open door on the other side. I had my hand wrapped in
his leash and went straight through after him, para-rolling
through the passenger bay, landing arse up on the ground on
the other side of the aircraft to the astonished looks of the
pilot. A big black door-gunner stared at me on the ground
before unbuckling and running over.

'Holy sheet, man, yo' fuckin' all right, man?'

'Yeah, okay. It's the dog, he likes helicopters. Does it a lot.'

Caesar was now sitting inside the chopper, a look of
innocence all over his face. I adjusted my pack and climbed in,
wishing I could choke the bloody mongrel. Bob leaned over
as we climbed up into the cool air. 'Do you think you could
break that bloody habit? Christ, sometimes it's embarrassing.'

Tracking Wing, 1966, Arthur Eather: 'What do you want, an easy life?'

The pilots were warrant officers, which surprised me as
all our chopper pilots were commissioned men. They had
caricatures painted on the back of their helmets, and one
showed the Coyote fucking the Road Runner. As we lifted
higher, one of them turned around to me with an anxious
look on his face. He shouted: 'Doesn't the dog like
choppers, buddy?'

I gave a thumbs up and Bob just rolled his eyes. The door-gunner was drumming his hands on his knees with his eyes tightly shut and obviously getting a dose of James Brown through his headset. I had noticed blacks, war and rock'n'roll seemed to go together.

NUI DAT, APRIL 1968

I woke up and walked outside the tent. It was still early morning and I decided to shave and shower before everyone else used all the hot water. The mirror still hung on the tree, and I looked at the face staring back. My cheeks were sallow and had sunk, along with my eyes, which were ringed with shadow. I had recently turned 20 years old, and I looked like a sick 50-year-old man. I felt chronically fatigued, it was an effort even to lather up, and when I did, instead of pulling a razor across my face, I lit up a cigarette and coughed for a few minutes. The short walk to the shower felt like a route march, and it was a struggle to lift the water into the canvas shower bucket.

ARRIVAL AT GROUND ZERO

North-west were the fire trails.

It hadn't taken long in country to work out what a fire trail was; a Vietnam War phenomenon, an outstanding example of the stupidity of the military, an irrational reaction to an enemy you couldn't see and who was dealing out all the shitty hands in the ground war.

Picture two huge D-8 bulldozers, called Rome Ploughs, spaced maybe 100 yards apart. Connect them with a ship's anchor chain, then find the biggest stretch of thickest jungle in the country. Put the drivers in steel-caged cabs, kick the monsters over and proceed forward under a black cloud of stinking diesel fume. Let them rip all day for a week.

Rip they do. With a clank, squeak and groan, they grind forward, taking down a million trees with that chain and massive blades. Greenery, wet lushness, tall timber that's been here for a thousand years comes down in an explosion of leaves. Root systems are ripped up, and every living thing within the forest flees for its life—including Charlie.

The Rome Ploughs turn and push the mess to the sides of the wide trail, turn, go back and dozer out any low bush that may have been missed during the anchor-chain demolition. After a few days or weeks of work, look back at the result, and there you have the fire trail: a swathe through the jungle not unlike the preparatory work for building a freeway.

The aftermath was a vision of an atomic bomb or meteorite blast that I had seen in pictures from the regions of outer Russia, where trees had been flattened in layers; a sort of Ground Zero in the war zone. Any man or animal travelling through the wilderness must at some stage cross a fire trail, like a hesitant child crossing the road. They will leave tracks, detectable from the air by a slow-moving Bird Dog, or recce aircraft, moving over for a routine early morning look-see. The logic is that the enemy can no longer move over large areas of forested country without being detected. The logic should also have held that the Viet Cong will crawl up to the edge of the forest and shoot the D-8 drivers, blast the Rome Plough and kill any other poor bastard wandering around in the clearing. Which they could, and did. And did again.

Ahead was the biggest fire trail I'd ever seen; it stretched horizon to horizon, and had cleaved through the thickest, tallest of jungles in the province. This was primordial stuff, a frenzy of trees and vines reaching up, clinging, climbing, grasping, building layer on layer, always struggling up to the sunlight until it formed green mats you imagined you could walk on.

The pilots had kept low on the northward flight. They now lifted, which gave us an overview of the jungle, the fire trail and, in particular, of a large cleared area which looked like a brown, ugly wound: a half-built fire base or half-completed camp surrounded by a dozen APCs—piles of rubbish, small fires burning and soldiers wandering around like ants over that familiar red-coloured earth.

This was part of the 3/5 Armoured Cavalry. It wasn't the sort of landing that sent our confidence soaring. The chopper swung down, hit the dirt and before we were off one side bodybags were being loaded in through the opposite door. I had never seen a bodybag before and I needed a cigarette. Now, quickly.

There were soldiers everywhere. Wandering around, lying about, smoking, eating out of ration cans, dozing next to an assortment of equipment: steel helmets, rifles, machine-guns, ammo belts and flak jackets. Music blared from the back of one APC, and a soldier was brushing his teeth while moving his body in tune to Marvin Gaye. He rinsed and spat out at the same time a short officer-type wearing a baseball cap walked over with his hand extended to Bob. There were soon smiles and greetings all round as more men milled around us, stroking the dog with 'Get us a gook, boy' and cigarettes were passed around. Someone offered me 'some cool shit'. I declined and lit up a Salem.

The officer began his explanation with, 'We have a situation here…' and finished it pointing down the fire trail.

Only on the ground did the enormity of the land clearance become apparent. The debris pushed to the flanks of the bulldozed area created mountains of smashed trees, roots with dirt hanging down like cooling lava, and in places earth had been mounded on the wreckage to create a parking ramp for an armoured carrier. The big .50 calibre machine-gun mounted on the APC pointed into the forest, with the gunner sitting back in his cupola, shirt off, sunglasses on.

The heap of weapons, the smoke from the fires, the rock music, these guys are just begging to be knocked over.

Inside of about 15 minutes we were in the back of an APC and rumbling off into the Great Unknown.

'The VC have hit twice in two days: rocketed the 'dozers, killed the drivers,' Bob explained, shouting into our faces while the carrier roared and heaved west to the contact area.

'We've been given a squad of GIs to go after the enemy from the last known position.'

Bill was already consulting his maps, orientating himself for the map-reading necessary after we entered the jungle.

Reliable Bill would pace off the yards with a sheep counter and use his compass to keep direction and distance. We had to know where we were at all times, and Bill's navigation would be critical. The Americans would likely do their own map-reading, but there was a question of accuracy, particularly if we hit a major force and needed artillery or gunships.

The carrier stopped, with a hiss the ramp dropped and we tumbled out. The support section was saddling up, and we began to climb over the huge tangle of smashed and shredded trees to get to the jungle while the APCs returned to the fire base. The support detail was a mixed bag: blacks and whites, some carried Armalites, others M60 machine-guns and M79s with the odd M72 rocket launcher here and there. Men wore flak jackets with no shirts, camouflage smocks with the sleeves ripped off and bush hats, or no hats at all. I was thankful there were no steel helmets, which made a hell of a thunk if they fell onto the ground.

One black soldier helped Caesar over the snarl of trees and branches. He was without doubt the biggest, meanest-looking man I'd seen in 'Nam. A piece of sweat-rag was wrapped around his head, he wore his flak jacket open and his torso shone with sweat over rippling muscles. The usual coloured beads hung around his neck, and he held an M79 in one hand while he pushed Caesar's bum up with the other. The voice was rich and deep.

'You Aussies know how to find these fuckers, right?' He stopped on top of the dirt and tree stumps like he'd just climbed a mountain and held his grenade launcher straight out in front of him.

'I'm called the Duper. You just find the motherfuckers, I'll waste 'em.'

Bob examined the area where the VC had launched the

RPG attack and took an unusually long time finding the track. He eventually gave me the thumbs up and I pulled the harness onto the dog.

'Six, seven, could be more,' Bob pointed to the beginning of a narrow trail. 'For sure they've shot off down there, and we'll be on a used foot trail most of the way I'd say, but there's probably loads of damn trails through this forest.'

He went back to the American officer and checked the radio was working. There was consultation over who was walking where, the distance between each man and a warning about being quiet.

He came back down to me. 'We're as ready as we're ever gonna be. Go!'

The war in Vietnam for the grunt was a slow slog. Stop, start, crouch, stand, walk, watch, listen. Minutes, hours, days of nothing but the same. Wet and hot, dry and hot, the forward scout crept along, either pushing his way through foliage or snipping his way carefully with a pair of secateurs. The men behind stopped, started, stopped, and all day breathed in hope that the scout wouldn't miss that sign, that sound, so he could get his Armalite up and fire before the opposition did.

At night, lie on the ground, eyes locked open until exhaustion forced sleep. Wake up and move forward again. Same bush, same trees, thoughts drifting, then brought back to the moment and place by a click of fingers from behind, or the snap of a bush to the front. Stop every 30 minutes for a smoke while a map check was carried out.

Back at the Infantry Centre in Australia there was a sign hanging on a tree that I'll never forget. It was in the area where we practiced patrol drills. As you walked slowly by, watching for non-existent enemy, you had to see it. Whoever put it in that precise location knew the world of the grunt. It burned into the mind:

'Tired Mate? Never Relax. Death Is So Permanent.'

GRUNTS AND COLD BEER

Two hundred yards into the canopy and we were all drenched in sweat, the sort that oozes out from both hard labour and nervous anticipation. Stinging rivers of the stuff were running into my eyes and I stopped for a moment to wrap my sweat-rag around my head. Shouldn't do this, I was once told, you can be mistaken for a Nog and get shot.

It was oppressive in here. Dead quiet. Not a shrill from a bird, no rustle through the low growth, even the lizards on the trees that normally called 'fuckyew' were quiet and still.

Caesar trotted on with his normal nonchalance. There was no strain on the tracking lead as the dog set his own easy pace. I heard Bob breathing and wheezing behind me. Fit as he was, the heat was sapping, and each breath was like sucking hot air from a furnace. He was covering me, watching the middle field, scanning left and right. A soldier with an M60 was immediately behind, 50-round belt on the gun, two more belts across his chest. Then came Bill, compass around his neck, plastic-covered map stuffed inside his shirt, sheep counter in one hand, SLR in the other. A dozen soldiers straggled out along the trail, and they were quiet.

We were soon setting a cracking rate, and the webbing was rubbing every sore and sorry spot on my skin. We had covered at least a mile. The forest was a web of trails and tracks that wound off left and right, weaving like a giant jungle circulatory system. The dog switched from one to the other like he was hooked to an invisible wire.

Suddenly Caesar reared up and back like he had been punched in the nose. I dropped to my knees, trying to get the rifle up, but it was so covered in sweat it fell. The dog looked at me foolishly, then I noticed the flick of the small snake on the track. Krait, deadly poisonous.

Bob was next to me. 'Did it bite him?'

I shook my head and Bob urged me on. I dry-croaked, 'Seek 'em, Caesar.'

About a click and a half and my concentration was starting to drift. It seemed to get darker and the forest thickened, but the trail remained well-defined beneath ferns which closed in at ankle level. I was thinking booby traps and trip wires when we broke out into a bomb crater. A B–52 bomb had come down through the canopy and blown a hole in the earth 15 yards wide. Caesar plunged down and up. *Tracking Wing, Confidence Course: 'Now let the dog loose, he'll go over. Let him go!'*

Too late. I was down on my knees, hands out, lead loose, rolling to the bottom of the hole and into water and stinking slime. By the time I scrambled up the other side Caesar was having another pee, tongue fully out and quivering.

'You smart bastard,' I hissed, grabbing at his lead.

I moved on 10 yards and squatted to allow the section to box around the crater and catch up. A drink for me and the dog, and a chance to catch our breath. Bob had taken a look at the trail and the earth around the bomb crater.

'They came straight through here. We're spot on. Hang on while Bill does some map work.'

Bob moved back into the shadows. I examined the dog. Seemed okay as far as the heat went. Bob gave the thumbs up.

The ground was rising as we passed the two-kilometre mark, and I felt the strain in the lead. A sudden point and I stopped as if I'd hit a wall. Listen, look. Nothing. Move on, and now I shortened the tracking lead. I felt a rush coming on. It was going to happen soon. What, I didn't know, but the words, the advice and the look on Arthur Eather's face was there in the final minutes. *'Don't just plough ahead…and watch for the bloody point.'*

The trail twisted again and Caesar lifted his head, picking up air hot with scent. All around just thick-trunked trees, low undergrowth of huge shining leaves and a few shafts of sun pooling across the track. The tracking lead jerked like a fast jag on a fishhook. The dog's ears shot up, and his shoulders hunched forward. A classic point and a sharp right bend in the track.

The Viet Cong was 50 yards to my right front, stretching his arms above his head and yawning. There was a clearing, three men at least, black and green uniforms and a machine-gun on the track facing me.

Scarcely able to breathe, I reeled Caesar back, keeping my eyes locked on the closest man. I shoved my arm out behind me and gave a thumbs down, *Enemy.* And I had them cold. The closest Viet Cong was frozen statue-still for several seconds, looking up through the tall trees to the sunlight.

It had been a textbook track from the fire trail to the VC camp. Silent, faultless, and the point had given me plenty of time to stop and ready the patrol for the kill. There Charlie stood and sat, like a bunch of men on a day's hike in the forest. Stopped for lunch—safe, secure. There was almost a temptation to call out and ask if we could join them. Caesar continued to stare at them. Not a muscle moved in the war dog's body. Did he know what we were going to do to them? Did he perceive them as enemy?

Bob crept past me and peered into the clearing. At that moment we both saw the mine, a command-detonated plate-sized explosive on three legs sitting to the side of the track. The VC may have been taking a smoko, but like any good soldier he had his security out, machine-gun and anti-personnel mine. But there was no sentry to give early warning.

Bob motioned to the man now behind me to swing the follow-up group to his right flank, extend and wait. There was rustle, shuffle and a few words spoken.

Fuck! The Viet Cong who was standing became aware of movement and stiffened. Bob had his SLR to his shoulder and fired. The man jerked up and flew backwards like he had stepped on a dozen marbles, and Bob fired again. Then the jungle exploded with a deafening crash. Tracers zipped through the bush, there was the rattle of M60, the short *braaatt* of an Armalite on automatic, shouts and yelling and a wall of fire.

I crawled back behind the biggest tree I could find and pulled Caesar in with me.

'There's a machine-gun on the track, Bob! *Watch it!*'

Bob fired again while I shouldered my rifle and thumbed the selector onto automatic. Stupid mistake—I emptied a full magazine in one breath. I slipped it off, took another from the basic pouch, put it on, bolt released, and set the selector to semi-automatic. From the kneeling position, I tried to pick the black against the green and snapped at targets as they presented.

'Stop, stop. *Cease bloody firing!*' Bob was up and moving forward, trying to assess the 30-second firefight.

But the Americans were having none of a cease-fire, and swept through the VC camp. I heard the *dupe* and *crump* of the M79 grenade launcher. *Hell, what was he firing at?* Moving into the clearing there was a trench, or firing pit, remains of a camp fire and stretchers. One man was writhing on the ground, red froth bubbling through a huge rent in his back. Another VC was crumpled half down another weapon pit, almost on top of a dead comrade, and rifles were scattered about. Bill found the mine cord and disconnected it. There was more heavy fire and Caesar jerked back in fright. Mr Duper, the big black grenadier, was walking casually back from the trail on the other side of the camp. His look was part smirk, part smile, and other soldiers were beginning to drift in with grins and high-fives.

Bob found the lieutenant.

'We need security here, fast. They'll be back.'

The officer ignored Bob. He was too busy examining the wounded VC. Then he said, 'We'll take him back for questioning.'

Several of us nearly had apoplexy.

'He's centre hit. He's a dead man, sir,' one soldier said, kicking at the enemy soldier.

'I don't believe this, but don't friggin' argue. Let's piss off, quick.' Bob spoke to Bill who had marked our contact on his map, while two men ripped up bits of the camp to make a stretcher. The VC machine-gun, a Browning automatic rifle, was retrieved and we moved quickly down the exit trail. Mr Duper, who hadn't stopped looking at me since the contact, had kicked the dead VC into the foxhole and now had one end of the litter with the wounded man lying spreadeagled on it.

Few words were spoken as Bob led us back down the jungle trail, using Bill's compass directions to navigate back to the fire trail. He didn't need it—Bob had his own built-in homing device, and ducked and weaved faultlessly along the trails. He picked up ammo belts and grenades dropped by the Americans on the way in. 'Good equipment retention, fellers,' he whispered during a breather.

I walked behind the stretcher party, with Caesar on his short lead. I was high with adrenaline, breathing in short gasps. The whole action was over in minutes; hit and run, just like Charlie.

'Now, *go.*' I looked up from the track to see Mr Duper suddenly twist the stretcher and hurl the wounded Viet Cong into the bomb crater. It was the one we had passed coming in, and the body rolled and twisted down to the bottom. The soldier scrambled down and made a pretence of checking the VC.

'Our WIA's a KIA, lootenant, sir,' he shouted up with a feigned look of concern on his face.

The American officer nodded with what seemed genuine regret and motioned Bob to press on. We picked up speed and were almost at a run by the time bright sunlight indicated the edge of the land clearing. There was the crackle of transmission on our radio confirming our locstat, and I heard the sound of carriers howling in the distance.

We broke out of the undergrowth and, sure enough, the Cavalry had arrived. There were whoops and yells of congratulations before Bob urged us to get on board and get out.

I was still jumping up and down inside my skin. So were a good many other men; taken over by the event, wild-eyed, pupils dilated. A few lit up a toke before the carriers wheeled and accelerated away.

I know why they were still called the Cavalry: they may have got rid of their horses, but they could still get several tons of bucking steel up to a fast gallop. Bits were flying from shelves, jerry cans were toppling loose, and I went from the bench seat to the floor and back again like a drunk, grasping straps or steel structures in an attempt to prevent smashing my brains out. I left the dog to his own devices and hoped he'd survive while I stood up to the main hatch and looked out.

A half a dozen APCs thundered across the land clearance. Two had confederate flags tied to their aerials, whipping in the wind—perfect targets for a VC with an RPG. On some of the speeding carriers men were riding on top with rags wrapped over their mouths. For a time men were boys, and the carriers roared up the fire trail, bouncing up and down from hillocks, flicking up rooster tails of mud. Another soldier was next to me, and I could just see Bob hanging out of the hatch of the carrier to my front when the first whoosh and flash erupted near the lead vehicle. Then another bang.

'*Ambush!*' my carrier driver yelled to his commander in the cupola next to me. In a bid to evade an incoming rocket, the vehicle swung sickeningly to the right flank, throwing me on top of Caesar.

The Cavalry knew something about tactics and went into counter-ambush drill, turning straight towards the forest edge to seize back the initiative. The big .50 calibres opened up along with small-arms fire from the troops on board. There was the ping and ricochet of enemy rounds striking the steel hulls of the APCs, and I saw the machine-gunner next to Bob buckle and fall inside the carrier. Another man grabbed his M60 but couldn't fire it. The Australian took the machine-gun, lifted the feedcover and plate and had the gun operating in less than half a minute.

The firing stopped and there was silence, then the hiss and crackle of a sitrep. One man WIA. Enemy KIA unknown. The engines revved up and the convoy made a fast run for home.

'Never been so happy to see this lot,' grunted Bob after we entered the stockade of heavy fighting vehicles. 'Keep your wits about you…and settle down.'

I was a shaking mess, and only realised when I grabbed Caesar that I must have emptied two magazines. The shells were on the deck of the APC, and the war dog was looking really pissed off about all the hot cartridge cases that had rained down on top of him.

'Got a wound, man…I got hit and I gotta good one. Got me a Purple Heart, man, got a trip outta here.'

The wounded American soldier was an hysterical and clownish sight, bleeding badly and almost crying with tears of relief while the medic tried to strip his fatigues and patch him up.

Bob and Bill went over to offer sympathy—and congratulations—while I scrounged a washbowl to water the dog.

The past hours had been a crazy trip, and I wondered if I had hallucinated it all. I tried to light a smoke, and only succeeded in singeing my eyebrows with the Zippo. Eventually puffing madly on the cigarette, I rubbed Caesar down with his brush when my big black friend, Mr Duper, sidled up and squatted next to me. He rolled a joint and looked at the animal.

'Damn good dog, tha's no shit. Clever lit'l fucker. What's he?'

'Labrador crossed with a kelpie. Mongrel.'

'*Mongrel!* Ain' no silly-assed mongrel. He's a *gook killer.*'

The soldier sat for a minute longer, dragging on the evil-smelling weed contemplating some deep thought, then said: 'You wan' sell your dog, man?'

The sounds of the chopper coming in put the dog on alert. I figured it was a resup—a resupply—or maybe the wounded GI was going out. No. It was tucker time, Yank-style: hot food, steaks, fries, ice cream and, incredibly, a crate of cold beer.

Bob came over. I asked if they were putting out a clearing patrol? 'Fuck, no, we don' do that. I hear they do clearance by fire, and I think I know what that means. But we'll just watch, okay?'

As the sun dropped a dozen APCs opened up with everything they had for what was known as The Mad Minute. A zillion rounds ripped into the jungle, tracers flicked crazily around the trees as the solid wall of fire trashed the bush through 360 degrees.

Silence. Night on the fire trail, and we offered to do sentry but the Cavalry wouldn't hear of it.

MAY TAO SECRET ZONE, NOVEMBER 1967

Somewhere between sleep and waking there was a dark region, and it was from there I woke with a start. For a second or two, panic, unable to recognise this bizarre place where I was sleeping. I checked the dog who was lying down but with his head twisted around, looking at me. I had that curious feeling that maybe comes to survivors after being involved a traumatic event: Why am I still here? Why am I here at all? What was the confluence of events that brought me here in the first place? Vietnam gave you choices, or no choices at all—a near miss or a hit and you're in a bodybag or eating steak with cold beer? A short trip in a Huey or into the back of an APC and you got out to a place where everyone was killing each other. Maybe that's why it was called the Funny Farm. Perhaps that's why everyone here wanted to get out.

Caesar started snoring again. For a long time during the night on the fire trail I couldn't close my eyes. There was the constant replay of an image: A young Viet Cong standing perfectly still, taking his last look up through the tall trees, bright sun shining on his face.

FIGHTS, CAMERAS, ACTION

Morning on the fire trail came with a sudden downpour, and men squatted under plastic lean-tos or inside carriers. A chopper was on its way with a 'maintdem'—a maintenance demand—which resupplied soldiers in the field with anything from replacement boots and fatigues, to spare M60 barrels and ripped and rotted webbing. The wear and tear on equipment and machinery was hellish during operations, worse in the wet, and maintdems were radioed through every few days, with replacements usually brought in on the next available chopper...maybe, perhaps.

The American commander was discussing with Bob and Bill the possibility of using trackers again. Seventh Battalion's dogs Justin and Tiber had also done a job with the 3/5 Cavalry, and now we had proved of value. The Australians were non-committal; we were a long way from Australian control, but if operations were in close proximity, and it was a joint operation, sure, why not? I reminded Bob later that he wasn't wrong about the 'joint' operation.

What the Americans lacked in fieldcraft they made up for with enthusiasm and firepower. There also were the steaks, ice-cream and beer to consider. The Iroquois landed and we piled on board.

'Hey, wait, man!' Mr Duper appeared at the door, and for the first time I saw a genuine smile. 'For your dog, buddy. He done good.' The soldier pushed the VC's captured Browning automatic rifle in. 'Charlie won't be needin' it, right?' He grinned, winked and rubbed Caesar's head, then was gone. We lifted and turned, and wobbled out over the fire trail.

Later someone hoisted the Browning above the bar in the

Support Company wet canteen, and secured it with special bolts. When I looked at it I didn't really take any pride in it as a trophy. I don't know why. I remembered more the angry black man called Duper who had forged a fast friendship with a black mongrel dog.

After four days of rest and recuperation leave in Vung Tau, we arrived back at Nui Dat suffering post-binge blues…and were told to get geared up for a major operation.

The 3rd Battalion (3RAR) had arrived at Nui Dat to join 2RAR and 7RAR. The Task Force was up to about 6000 men. Lyndon Johnson was pouring more American troops into the ground war, Vietnam had long since passed guerilla and counter-insurgency status, and divisions of NVA were pouring into the South. We were re-rationed, re-ammoed and briefed, then told to wait.

Caesar had his bowl in his mouth when I arrived at the kennels in the afternoon, and Marcus was flat on his back, sleeping with his legs in the air. I divided the meat, which had been sprinkled with chopped vegetables, and broke two packets of biscuits over the meals.

'You blokes get it easy—fresh beef, free air travel, walks in the scrub. Every day it's things to do, places to go.' I crept up on Marcus and shouted 'Bang! Contact front!'

Marcus came awake with a start, looked at me then at Caesar. *Your handler's gone loopy again, old dog. Talking to himself and thinks the war's a bit of a holiday. Should try sleeping on a cold bedboard every night.*

Fergie was asleep, so I decided to do the feed and walk, letting both dogs out for their nightly run. They took off like missiles, heat-seeking through the rubber. Marcus's ears were pinned back as he executed a tight turn, his tongue hanging out, eyes wild with the excitement of freedom. Caesar disappeared then reappeared at full speed, before screeching to a halt, investigating a new smell.

I smoked watching the pair. It had never occurred to us what the future held for the two war dogs. I tried again to recall if anyone had ever said anything about the subject of the dogs' return to Australia. I wondered what handlers Norm and Tom were thinking over at 7RAR—they were getting short in country, with only about a month left. What would happen to Justin and Tiber?

Two days into the new operation and Victor Company of the 1st Battalion Royal New Zealand Infantry Regiment ran full on into a contact with the NVA. In the thick bush, with darkness falling, 20 Kiwis took on a platoon of enemy. It was Deep Serious for the New Zealanders, who had been brought from Malaysia to fight in Vietnam alongside the diggers from 2RAR. For the Kiwis it was a case of another strange country, another strange jungle. Somebody else's war.

The fight was fast, bloody and violent, with neither party prepared to pull back. It was rocket fire, AK-47s, shouts, screams and flat-on-the-guts, arse-tightening time with the Kiwis—who fought with the intensity of street brawlers — locked up against seasoned Communist jungle fighters. 2RAR Battalion Command desperately tried to get a reinforcement company across to the contact, but thick bush, buggered men and darkness meant the fight went on for five bloody hours. Old US Dakotas came and filled the air with flares. Gunship teams sent down a stream of hot lead and 40mm canon fire. It was packin' death time.

Morning: 10 NVA bodies, plenty of blood trails, two friendlies wounded. It had been hot, close contact which went simply on the Contact File Report as having had 'a reasonable outcome'. Early afternoon of the same day and Fergie and I saddled up for two tracks. Fergie and Marcus went out on the first Huey to Victor Company, and I struggled with my mad dog and got on board the second chopper for a re-run with the 3/5 Cavalry.

The cowboy at the controls was obviously a frustrated Phantom pilot. I had secured a seat, and Bob sat on the floor for a hair-raising ride of sharp banks at just above treetop level. It is virtually impossible to fall out of a helicopter, door-gunner Scotty had once told me; the forces created during flight are both gravitational and centrifugal, ensuring you stay locked to the seat or steel deck. I reckon Scotty was drunk when he told me that story—the violent motions now inside the Huey took Caesar perilously close to one open door and then wobbling over to the other. The war dog considered this a hoot. His handler contemplated the size of the A4 charge sheet if the Army's valuable investment vanished into the void.

A Cobra gunship scooted past us, the turbo-charged, sleek machine was likely on its way to the Cavalry position along with us. I exchanged looks with my visual tracker: Americans…contact with the enemy…gunships. Bob shot back a look: *Don't dwell on it, one mental breakdown at a time.*

The pilot banked left then swung to starboard and made for a clearing like he was landing a B-52. Bob and I braced ourselves for the smash. The skids dug into soft earth and the pilot turned to give us the thumbs up. 'We're here guys. *Get Some!*'

I was out, trying to handle the dog and hoist my pack at the same time as trying to avoid the tail rotor while the crazy pilot spun the machine and headed for the tree line. 'Okay, so there's hurry and really hurry up, but he was trying to break Vietnam air speed records,' I muttered to Bob while we made our way to the closest APC.

It wasn't thick jungle around here, just horrible, clinging shoulder-high bush and the occasional banana tree. I examined the dirt, not red, more black, and quite dry. Not much moisture to aid scent tracking. In a few minutes Bob trotted back.

'They've had a straight-out contact with half a dozen VC. RPG and rifle fire. The enemy's bugged out and we'll follow up with infantry and carriers bringing up the rear. Let's go!'

Bob located the track from obvious ground signs and disturbance left in the earth by men making off at a high rate of knots. I harnessed up and waited to go. Ten minutes later I was still waiting. 'What's the bloody hold up?'

Bob queried behind him then said: 'They reckon they have to get more people in position. Don't ask me what that means.'

With Caesar in harness I didn't like to delay. The fact he was strapped in indicated to the dog he was now working. We weren't working. I lit up a smoke.

'Go!' Bob closed up and I saw men behind him ready at last. Caesar shot off into a banana grove, had a leak, cast around for smell and pushed on. There were more banana trees as we went further, and I felt cool and relaxed. I noticed some of the trees had a good head of fruit on them.

Caesar suddenly shot back with a jerk and low growl. At the same time, a man stepped out in front of us. As I brought the rifle up I clearly saw he had something on his shoulder, but I didn't fire. Why I didn't shoot I just don't know, my selector was on semi-automatic. Bob didn't fire either, possibly because I didn't open up first. The man lowered the equipment from his shoulder, and I recognised it as a hand-held movie camera. He was a cameraman, and had been sent up front to film us. I had been a breath away from killing him. In such a weird situation I did what any digger would do—sat on my arse, clenched my teeth and lit a smoke.

Bob glared at the man who identified himself as a South Korean newsman. He was hardly fazed by the fact he was a heartbeat away from being blasted into the Great Network In The Sky. Bob let him have it.

'I dunno who you are or how you got here, but you were nearly zapped. Nearly bloody dead, *you stupid shit!*'

Bob grabbed the man by the collar and flung him back into the arms of the approaching American.

'Shoot him if you like, we nearly did.'

I took the harness off to show Caesar he had stopped tracking and gave him a drink. 'Thanks for the point, idiot!' The dog looked up at me with that disconcerting stare that said: *'I only point at enemy, not a Korean cameraman with a death wish. And you're the idiot!'*

Still shook up, I started again, but couldn't get into a rhythm, and we trotted on through more banana plantations. I began to suspect we were near habitation, but the dog gave no point, just head down, ground scenting. Maybe he was in a sulk with me over my growling at him?

I passed a freshly cut tree, then another, and more. Trees cut? Camps? Bunkers? Enough. I pulled up and whispered to Bob. 'I reckon there's something up front—village, bunker complex, definitely something, but Caesar's not pointing.'

Bob consulted maps with the platoon commander. Topographical maps showed nothing and aerial photo charts showed thick cover broken by the odd clearing. No spots indicating old buildings. The decision was made to bring up the infantry soldiers and carriers and make a wide sweep.

I unharnessed the dog as the first Americans passed through, and I felt comfortable with the fact they seemed professional; quiet, disciplined, no chatter or radios crackling, just chewing gum and wide grins. I didn't see my mate Mr Duper this trip.

'Fire in the hole!' The shout rang out and I thought I was in the movies. *Maybe we're making a war film.* There was a thump and black smoke rising. I hit the ground and pushed the dog into a bush, at the same time taking a fire position.

'Fire in the hole!' More thumps.

'That's the first time I ever heard that,' Bob was grinning at me. 'Real war stuff!'

We gathered up and moved forward. Fifty yards, maybe less, and we were in a VC village—more an encampment with stretchers in trees, tables and chairs constructed from jungle timber and trapdoors to tunnels and hides. Several trapdoors were open and grenades were going in 10 to the dozen, followed by 'Fire in the hole!' Thump, thump, thump, the concussion shook the ground and brought down leaves and deadfall. I found a shady spot on top of a bunker and sat down for a smoke and poured water into a canteen for Caesar. I suddenly thought how far I'd come in this war. I was a month from my twentieth birthday, nearly eight months in country, and I was sitting on top of a VC bunker having a smoke. Familiarity breeds indifference.

It wasn't long before the whole circus arrived. APCs rumbled in, hatches flew open and radios tuned into Marvin Gaye and The Supremes. Cases of cold flavoured milk were unloaded. Sucking back the milk, I noticed my photographer friend filming me with the dog. 'You're still alive then, you crazy fucker?' He smiled, nodded and moved away. I stood up and called after him.

'You have to pay when you film Australian war dogs, you know that don't you?' It didn't work, all I got was another stupid grin. It wasn't remotely possible he was working with the Yanks, making a movie, and the wait at the start of the track was so he could get into position? Naw, they wouldn't do that...?

Standing I caught the smell, the odour of enemy, the pungency that hangs around near Viet Cong camps. It was smell that stayed with you, that comes back when you least expect it. They smell us too, a soldier once told me. 'We think they stink, they reckon we do. Interesting, isn't it?'

It was late afternoon when the American chopper came in. The aircraft landed with the regulation steak and fries. We were offered a backload to our fire support base. For a minute we considered pulling a fast one and staying the night, just for the food. Bob said we better go.

NORTH-WEST PHUOC TUY, 1967

In a chopper or an APC you get a minute to think; let your mind drift away from the place, despite the smell of stale sweat, the clunk, groan and squeak of the carrier, or the drumbeat of blade chopping air.

I stroked Caesar's head and recalled a quiet house in a working-class suburb. It was my parents' home, and dad's dog was chasing a ball. Normalcy, I told myself, you should try to cling to things you remembered as normal. Like the letter in the top pocket of my shirt. It shouldn't have been there, you weren't allowed to carry personal mail in the scrub. I must have forgot, and I touched it now. It was stained with red dirt, and a lot of the writing had smudged from rain and sweat, but I remembered a few of the lines which my old girlfriend had penned weeks ago. 'Hope you're safe over there...I lit a candle in church for you. Please write when you have time. I know how busy you must be.'

BITES AND BARKS

Polly and his war dog, Julian, had been in country with 3RAR about three weeks. Julian, along with fellow dog Janus and handler Phil, had not yet been called out on a track, and they were busting to hear how things had gone with us when they dropped around to 2RAR Tracking Team lines.

I had been looking forward to seeing another dog handler; I was going a little stir crazy. Ken was out of the tent a lot of the time, hanging out with Simon most of the day. Diggers in war tended to attach themselves to a partner, hang together in Nui Dat and on operations. As dog handlers, Fergie and I would have paired off, but we were, through operational necessity, often split up and didn't have a chance to create that soldiers' mateship with a fellow digger. In the jungle on ops, on a fire base or patrolling with a rifle company, most of the time I was on my own, or paired up with a different soldier on each occasion. My closest friend was a black dog, a mute.

Polly was a guy I had become firm friends with in Sydney. He eventually overcame the acne problem, and apparently convinced the quacks he would be okay in the tropics, spots or no spots. After the 'acne-scraping incident' with Armidale Tex, I hung out with the pair. I hadn't seen or heard of Polly since I was posted to 2RAR.

The exuberant Polly loved music and women, and spent his nights socialising at the nurses' quarters in Ingleburn playing Walker Brothers and Gene Pitney LPs. He'd stagger back to the Tracking Lines, hang onto the end of his bed with an imaginary whip, and yell 'Mush, my huskies. Mush!' After crossing the Alaskan wilderness, he'd crash forward onto his cot and pass out. Polly had been breaking his neck to get into the war. He'd made it.

A vet check for Julian, Janus, Caesar and Marcus had been arranged, and early morning we jumped into the back of a long-wheelbase Land Rover for the trip to Vung Tau.

'They working you much since you been here?' Polly had Julian leaning over his shoulder, sucking in the wind, while Caesar was doing the same, slobbering over me.

'Don't want to turn you off,' I answered, 'but this place is fucking hopeless. Delta Company's been good on call-outs. The problem with the others is they'll stomp all over a friggin' contact area looking for Nogs then think, "Stuff, we can't find anything. Call the trackers." We are flown in and the trail's buggered. Fergie's had real problems like that.'

On the road to Vung Tau there was a chance to see the pre-war Vietnam: farmers, fishermen, buses held together by string and wire and loaded down with humanity, pigs and chickens. There were actually smiles and waves for Australian soldiers in this semi-safe zone.

'This place ain't Bulli, Helensburgh,' I went on. 'It's full of fucking weirdos. Everything puts shit on you or bloody blows you up. I wandered into a minefield, twice. Went out with a bunch of gung-ho Yanks, twice, and one then offered to buy the dog. Oh, nearly forgot, I tried to shoot Fergie in the head and then filled sandbags for two weeks. Tell you something, Polly, if you get a call-out to a place called the Long Green, stick your finger in the light socket and save yourself the grief.'

Fergie nodded agreement and chipped in, 'And if you run out of Aussie piss, you gotta drink some shit called Schlitz or Blue Ribbon.'

Caesar turned to look at me and I got a face full of his

spit. 'The dog's still chopper troppo. It drives me bloody mad, but there's no cure for him, and I've learnt to live with it. Sometimes it gives me the absolute shits. Nearly had a rotor through the brain I don't know how many times.'

I noticed Polly was staring at Fergie and then looked back at me. 'You know, you blokes look really bad. I shit you not, you look half-starved, thin as fucking rakes and you're going a sort of yellow colour. You're starting to look almost bloody Vietnamese.' He laughed. We didn't. It wasn't funny getting told you looked like what you felt.

The American vet and his assistant Chris recognised me from my first visit, when we'd arrived in the country and had the dogs checked. I introduced the 3RAR team, then we swapped banter on how much time we had left and whether we'd extend in country. This was a standard American joke. US troops could stay on after their year's tour—no sane soldier would, but some did. Their mental condition was scrawled on the front of their helmet: *High On War.*

The vet weighed and examined the dogs, trimmed their nails, cleaned their ears and brought the shots up to date. There were about 2000 American war dogs in Vietnam, and the US Army had its own Veterinary Corps. War vets were posted all over South Vietnam, treating scout dogs, sentry dogs, canines that went into tunnels and those who detected mines. There were also at least four American Combat Tracking Teams using labradors. We had been told there was a VC bounty on dog handlers, and about 100 American dog handlers were already dead.

'Seen our new attack dog?' asked the vet. 'He's one mean son-of-a-bitch.'

Dogs treated at the vet centre for war injuries were kept overnight in kennels at the back of the main clinic. I'd seen them on a previous trip, and found it difficult to believe there were so many canines in the war. At Long Binh they actually had a dog hospital where a team of vets patched up wounds and did reconstruction surgery.

'Chris, show the Aussies our latest patient.'

We all walked down the kennel block, then entered a narrow passageway. Chris picked up a stick with one end mangled like it had been stuck under a tank track. At the end of the tunnel was an enclosure with a dog box in the shadows. The name of the animal was scrawled on cardboard and attached to the gate: 'SATAN.'

Chris banged the stick on the heavy-duty arcmesh. 'Hey, Satan!' Not a sound or movement. Chris stuck the wood inside the cage and turned to us.

'Now watch. *Satan, Get Some!*'

The dog came out of his box like a missile and slammed against the mesh several feet above the ground. The real size of the dog was obscured by a set of jaws and teeth that hooked into the steel, then dropped to the wooden pole and ripped across the timber like a bandsaw. Froth flew through the wire and we all started back like we had touched an electric fence.

The power and bulk of the enormous German shepherd, coupled with the sheer malice on its face, for a moment struck us dumb.

'*What the fuck is that?*' Polly shouted above the roar coming from the kennel.

The bark was enough to trigger a heart attack; what this monster could do with its bite if it broke down the gate was the stuff of nightmares.

'You've just got to use the right words, otherwise he's as gentle as a kitten,' Chris smiled with assurance.

'Oh yeah, fuck you, *and fuck 'im, too.*' Polly was looking at the attack dog in disgust.

'If he's like that when he's sick, what the bloody hell does he do when he's fit and well?' queried Fergie, peering around the edge of the gate.

I had to ask the Dumbest Question In The World: 'What's he used for?'

Chris gave me a look, smiled and we walked out of the kennel block. 'The Army's preparing a whole new type of war dog—a real fucking killer. We figure when the VC start the big offensive we're goin' to release 200 Satans out in the boonies. War'll be over in a week.' The American was the only one who laughed.

We left the dogs in the kennels for a couple of hours and had a few drinks at the Beachcomber Club before driving back to Nui Dat. Polly told us about life at the Tracking Wing and how training was going, then reeled off his favourite mad dog jokes. Satan left an impression—a bad one about attitudes by certain armed force to their K9s. There were dogs trained for brutal behaviour, and some were trained by brutal people. There were also dogs who scouted ahead of patrols and were the first to become a casualty; cost effective warfare where the dog died, not the man. I didn't think for a minute this applied to most dog handlers in the war. There were those American war dogs who, like Caesar and Marcus, were cared for, appreciated, even loved. After a few hours with an old friend like Polly, and retrieving Caesar from his holding kennel at the vet, I felt good again.

'What's the biggest, meanest dog you've ever seen?'

It was evening mealtime in the steel shed next to the company cookhouse, and I was sitting with Simon, Twiggy, JC and Ken. Twiggy was squinting and bitching about the

US-brand chilli sauce that was put out on the table every night with other condiments, including a repulsive red goo called Catsup.

'You could use this crap to clean the drains. Hey, maybe we could spray it on the Nogs. Bad dogs? Had a Doberman near our place who once caused the posties to blackban the whole street.'

Simon came alert at the reference to 'postie' and piped in.

'We heard from a rifle company bloke that anyone who goes home has to beat the living shit out of any bloody postie. They've banned delivery of all Vietnam mail going home.'

Twiggy gave a super squint. 'You're shittin' us, right?'

'No, it's a protest against the war.'

Protest? It was a word we hadn't come to grips with, but there was a feeling of unease around the Task Force that the war wasn't popular anymore. AFVN Radio was carrying nothing about protests in America, and the only word coming into Nui Dat was from letters back home— demonstrations, debates by long-hairs. The thing was that the groundswell could boost enemy morale; boost it to the extent they would launch a major offensive.

'When it comes, it'll be on their Lunar New Year, February,' said JC who knew everything. 'It'll be a Some-thing Big.'

Ken nodded with a grin. 'Right. And put money on it, Charlie's going to drop a huge dump right on us.'

SONG BA DAP, PHOUC TUY, JULY 1967
— PART 1

Caesar and Marcus were having a ball. The game was called 'See How Long You Can Balance On An Armoured Personnel Carrier Seat Before Being Thrown Onto Your Arse'. The game was in progress while the dogs' handlers were ready to puke from the fumes and thump and roll of the APC. Driven by twin tracks, the carrier took on every small tree in its path: rammed it, climbed it, pushed it over, then slithered down the other side. The effect on those inside the steel hull was a sickening, tumbling ride, tossed from one wall to the other.

'Hey, reverse, fuckwit. I think you missed a tree back there,' Fergie abused the driver and the APC commander standing in the turret above us. The driver, visible from the shoulders down, was working the steering lever and kicking the pedals, forcing the machine farther into the forest. Ahead somewhere lay an enemy camp which had only hours ago been pounded by artillery fire and strafed by gunships. Trackers were moving up to recce the area and follow up any VC who had bugged out.

The method of deployment was by carrier, the worst of all possible transport in Vietnam. Walking with blisters all over your feet was preferable to 'going in by tracks'. In an APC you saw nothing and felt everything. Encased in the steel hull, the conversation always got around to How Many Ways Can You Get Killed In A Carrier? Would a bullet from an AK penetrate the side? There was no debate a satchel charge tossed through the hatch would kill you, a mine could rip out the floor, which was packed with sandbags against such an event, and fucking sure a rocket would knock a hole in it. But it was the inability to sit, stand or squat while you groaned and creaked across rugged terrain that led to the most number of curses you could summon in any given minute.

The dogs had the advantage of four legs and could trampoline from floor to seat and back, like what the two buggers were doing now. It was a new game they could play all day.

'I can't stand any more of this shit,' Fergie yelled picking himself up off the deck and trying to push Marcus's arse out of his face. I felt the APC begin to tilt up and back. The driver had picked on a tree that wasn't going to budge, and the machine howled then slid sideways down an incline. I grabbed at Caesar and a loose nylon strap.

'Brace yourself, grit your teeth, we're going over!'

For a moment a Studebaker at Bulli Pass in the rain flashed through my mind. Then the APC righted itself, a tree crashed across the top and a branch splintered downwards through the open hatch. At the same time a huge red ants' nest burst open on the floor.

'Oh, shit, no!' Fergie grabbed Marcus and pulled him up onto the seat the same time the ants spread outwards like an attacking force across the floor, onto our boots then onto our legs and up our arms.

I shouted at the driver who was desperately trying to slam his machine into reverse. This only caused all the foliage inside the carrier to thrash around like clothes in a spin-drier, tossing the red ants into the air. I felt the first bite then another and another…Fuck Vietnam, fuck the jungle, fuck these fucking ants.

SOMETHING BIG COMES BY

Australian military operations were largely confined to Phuoc Tuy province in 1967. We chased the VC on search-and-destroy missions; they thumbed their noses then ambushed us or blew us up. We took ground in the day; they moved back in at night. We relocated the populace to safe havens and 'new life' villages; Charlie came in and shot the 'liberated'. We chased them, tracked them, killed them, tallied the body count…and military command felt that, by and large, we had secured our Tactical Area of Responsibility.

Wrong again. Just how wrong became evident in January 1968 with the launch of Operation Coburg, the first time the Task Force would move out of Phuoc Tuy province. There was continuing intelligence that the enemy—NVA, Viet Cong, Rocket Regiments and trained sappers—were planning an all-out attack on the giant American bases of Long Binh and Bien Hoa, as well as Saigon itself. The Australians were ordered by the American command to move into the Long Kanh-Bien Hoa provinces border area and put down a blocking force. Nearly 2000 men from the 2nd and 7th Battalions and Task Force HQ packed for the long haul north.

On 24 January we grabbed the dogs, sandbags of rations, donned flak jackets and helmets and scrambled onto the back of trucks for the butt-busting road convoy up Route 15. Our destination was a fire base and maintenance area established by the American 199 Brigade. The Anti-Tank boys, along with the Trackers, flew up by Chinook and Iroquois. Fergie and I sat in trucks with Caesar and Marcus; not so much sat as clung on for dear life atop tarpaulin-covered loads. It was like riding on a trampoline, but you did get a chance to observe the locals.

We raised clouds of dust in the villages, splashed through washaways and meandered through an endless quilt of rice fields and peasant villages. The last hamlet we drove through was called Xa Trang Bom, and it stuck in my mind that they were a sullen, hostile little lot. They stared up at us in the trucks, eyes dulled of expression that gave off bad vibrations; we weren't wanted in their little village.

To the war dogs it was a ride in the open air. Caesar stood up with his paws on the truck cabin, the shorter-legged Marcus tried the same position but slipped back on his arse every time the lorry rocked or slammed over a pothole.

The fire base was just one click past Xa Trang Bom. The grunts of the 199th were moving out, leaving a sea of trash: squashed ration cartons, pieces of personal equipment and rotting cans of food. I wandered up to the latrine and retreated, gagging. Weapon pits and bunkers were caving in, or still in a state of half-construction, and corrugated 'hardbacks', which were half-circle cylinders of steel used as overhead cover, were buckled and broken.

Everywhere sandbags were busted and scattered. The place was a rubbish tip—but it was also home for a week or more, and we had about two hours before dark to get below ground in some sort of comfort. I teamed up with two Administration Company men and we decided to buddy-up and clean out a machine-gun bunker position for ourselves. Fergie had found a spot on the other side of the perimeter, and during the digging he came over with Marcus.

'We found a grenade in our hole, pin out and clip just held on with black tape. You want it?'

The soldier with me stuck his head out of the bunker,

holding something at arm's length. 'Give you a half-used toilet roll for it.'

Among soldiers anxiety transferred by osmosis; there was a bad smell here, and it wasn't all coming from the over-full shit pits. We dug on like men possessed. I filled sandbags while my two mates cleaned out and widened the weapon pit into a fair-sized bunker. We packed on overhead cover, and cleared the ground for fields of fire down to the single roll of perimeter wire.

Just before dark we took a break. There hadn't been a single grizzle about the work we had to do; it was an unspoken *just fucking do it.* You only had to look at what was happening in and around the fire base to note everyone had got the message; dig, dig and more digging in. Choppers came and went all day. The sky over the operational area was full of Iroquois ferrying men in, Skycranes and Chinooks slung 105 artillery pieces, gunships banked and weaved, small glass-bubbled Sioux and super-fast Coyotes base-hopped with men, maps and briefing papers. I remember the words back at the Dat: 'Something Big.'

I took Caesar down to the wire for a crap, and noticed two huge American 155 self-propelled guns being backed into a position very close to our bunkers. They were beyond the wire and had their own self-contained location, but even at a distance the juggernauts were awesome. They looked like a conventional tank, but had a massive barrel that some joked could throw a shell from Saigon to Darwin.

They also had the most effective anti-personnel shell in Vietnam; a canister that fired from the gun burst and scattered hundreds of pieces of chopped steel rod at muzzle velocity into any approaching enemy. A member of the gun crew had his shirt off and was whistling to himself while pushing a large brush down the barrel like a chimney sweep. I thought to myself, *hope those blokes don't traverse too far right*—if the concussion generated by their blast passed over our bunker, it would have us taking aspirin for the rest of our lives.

We waited for a call-out.

From day one, 2RAR went into contact with the enemy. The 25-set radio in our bunker crackled continuously as Australian platoons went up against NVA regulars, bunkers were hit, firefights triggered and ambushes sprung. By January 31, four battalion members were dead and 15 had been wounded and dusted off.

Choppers ran an around-the-clock service out of the fire base, and we loaded rations, water, clothing and ammunition. At night we hunkered down in the bunker, but I refused to sleep in the hole, so I jerry-built a sleep-out from a hardback and sandbags where Caesar and I could crawl in together. I figured if we were mortared, we could tumble and roll into the bunker with the other two men.

It was exhausting work on the base, but we took some consolation we weren't patrolling across the main attack routes being used by the NVA and Viet Cong. At night we shared watch on the M60 and waited.

Soon after midnight on February 1 the war exploded across Vietnam. The enemy launched the Tet Offensive, simultaneously striking at every major base and city in the South; hoping the massed attacks would swing the war in their favour in terms of body count and winning the hearts and minds of the South Vietnamese.

The radio, along with a field telephone, spewed out a continuous stream of transmission; urgent short messages that claimed Saigon had been hit, Long Binh, Bien Hoa, towns around the Task Force back in Phuoc Tuy, and, up north, from Hue to the DMZ, the Demilitarised Zone, and back down to the Mekong Delta.

From where we were positioned the blackness over the distant military bases became day, with aircraft dropping a curtain of paraflares. Puff The Magic Dragon, an aircraft with miniguns, rained sheets of fire down into the enemy, while every howitzer in the province went into overdrive.

The Australians in our operational zone braced themselves for major fights with NVA/VC assault units withdrawing from the battlefields around Saigon.

We watched liked spectators at Guy Fawkes for a few minutes, then there was the crack made by rounds from small-arms fire when they passed over head.

'Jesus wept, it's on!' The digger sitting next to me climbed behind the M60 and began to lay the belts out on the sandbags.

'Get the dog in here, Peter. I reckon we could get some shit.'

I pulled Caesar down into the blackness of the hole and stashed two flak jackets at the bottom of the pit, encouraging the dog to lay on them. 'Gonna be a long night, boy, keep your doggy head down.'

I was shrugging into my webbing, when I heard a hiss from the soldier on the gun. 'Something moving...coming up through the trees.'

Peering through the Starlight scope at the unreal, dreamy, green and yellow generated by the instrument, I imagined I could see figures moving, but wasn't sure. Then I was. For certain: two, three, four men, hunched, walking slowly forward.

The next second the viewfinder flashed white, almost blinding me. It seemed like a thunderflash had gone off in the weapon pit. Every man threw his hands up to his ears at the detonation and felt a thump on the back of his head, like someone had walloped us with a baseball bat.

Another thunderflash and Caesar let out a strangled cry. I jumped over to the dog and wrapped my arms around him. The dog was terrified, ears flat, mouth open, and shaking uncontrollably. *Fuck, we're being mortared!* But there was no slap of shrapnel and no blood…yet.

The flash and bang came again, the weapon pit shook as if hit by a mini earthquake. The radio crackled on: 'Three out…canister…wait.'

My ears cleared and I was sure I heard a loudhailer coming from outside. Then when the next flash went off, the realisation hit me. 'It's those bloody mobile guns—they're firing canister down at the tree line.' I shouted at the closest man next to me. The concussion wave was passing out and over our gun pit.

I struggled to make my way up and scream at the bastards when another bang sent me down on top of the dog, who was going berserk trying to get out of the hole. I wrapped my arms and legs around him. Then there was silence, but no one could speak.

Sit quietly, sweat and wait. Three men and a dog. A bunker on a scrubby hill. A full war raging on the horizon.

The fire support base and Task Force maintenance area seemed to be in the eye of a storm, with companies from 2RAR and 7RAR in major contact all around us. Flareships were cluttering the sky in the east where several big battles were underway, and they created a scene that in any other place at another time would almost be festive. The illumination from the flares when they drifted downwards caused a fast shift in the shadows across our front. You thought for a minute someone was moving out there, and then realised it was a tree changing shape. Another flare, another group of phantom enemy moving up. Darkness again and then the process repeated itself—all night.

Thank God, though, the 155s had stopped firing. Caesar was still in the grip of a shaking fit, and I worried the gun blast had damaged his ears. I crawled down next to him and rubbed his coat and stroked his head. It had some effect, because by the time dawn broke through he was up the front on the bunker with his front paws on the sandbags.

The four of us crawled out into an overcast morning, and it took more than a minute or two to absorb the damage caused by the canister rounds. The anti-personnel shot had blasted every leaf from every tree to the front of the gun position. It seemed the ground without vegetation had been swept clean with a broom and the chopped metal rods had then stripped the thickets. The effect was as if more than a hundred skeletons of trees now held their arms to the sky in mock surrender.

'Will you look at that,' the digger next to me whistled, and then we walked over to the barbed wire near the guns where four Americans were smoking and drinking coffee. We decided to have a dig, and I called out. 'You blokes provide ear protection before you shoot?'

A Yank put his hand to his ear. Another digger called out. 'Do you have any spare earplugs?'

More hands to ears. Then one of the gunners grinned and pointed out beyond the wire across to the devastation in the tree line. *'Got some!'*

'I suspected it, they're all fucking deaf as newts. Might as well talk to a sandbag.' The soldier next to me had gone quiet and was gazing off to the bare trees. He nudged me:

'Do you reckon you can see in that tree what I think I can see?' I looked hard in the direction he was pointing with his rifle. Something was gently moving in the upper branches. It was a piece of a shirt or trousers. From one leg, if it were trousers, there was clearly a single boot sticking out.

The soldier looked at me. 'Couldn't be, could it?' He blew air out of puffed cheeks. 'The buggers were really here, up on the wire. A probe maybe?'

Still contemplating the possibility the VC had tried a night break-in at the fire base, we started breakfast. Fergie wandered over with Marcus and we took a walk around the perimeter wire.

Later that day a company-sized enemy unit attacked Xa Trang Bom and we went below ground again while Delta Company began street-to-house fighting only a 1000 yards away. Next day the contacts intensified and we began loading choppers again. The radio transmission continued with a frantic cackle of contact, WIAs, KIAs, dustoffs and calls for artillery support.

The Tet Offensive took a grip, and the country was on fire. We were warned we'd be hit in the next few nights.

An officer came down from the echelon and stuck his head under the hardback. I was rummaging around for a suitable lunch. I wasn't hungry, in fact I'd felt sick in the guts for days, but decided to try and force down turkey loaf, peaches and crackers with Vegemite.

'We're moving back to Nui Dat tomorrow by road convoy. 3RAR's coming in. Pass it on to the others, will you?'

We cleaned up that afternoon and got ready to go home. I pulled myself up for a moment and looked at Caesar. 'Where is home, old mate?' After eight months or more, what really *was* home? A hill in Long Kanh? A tent in Nui

Dat? A house in a quiet suburb where my mother and father lived? I wondered what they were seeing and hearing about the events of the past week.

Three days after we arrived back at Nui Dat the enemy hit the fire base and nearly overran it. The Americans and 3RAR forced them back, but they came two nights later and got in between the wire separating the 155s and the main-tenance area. Packin' death time for the Australians again. I wondered how Polly and Julian had settled in at the shit hole we had left? How had the pair handled the assault? How had they dealt with the half-deaf Yankee gunners? Silly bugger, Polly. It'd be good to see him when got back and swap war stories. I could see him now with, 'Fine fuckin' mess you left us in. You piss off and the real shit hits us.'

The Anti-Tank and Trackers had gone through a major contact and killed seven NVA in a savage fight during Operation Coburg. Maybe that's why things were so quiet down the lines. Nothing brings sobriety and quiet contem-plation more than looking the grim reaper right in the face—and getting out with your balls intact. 2RAR killed 181 of the enemy, and seven 2RAR Aussies died during the three-week Operation Coburg. Across the country the enemy had died in their thousands during the Tet Offensive. And it was still on.

Time dragged: raking leaves, TAOR (tactical area of respon-sibility) patrols and a spell in Nui Dat. I wrote letters and checked the calendar in the tent, a nude with the months, weeks and days across her body. I went outside and lit up a smoke when I noticed a soldier making his way down the lines, peering in tents, obviously looking for someone.

'You Trackers?'

'Yeah.'

'You know the Trackers at 3RAR?'

I stood up, suddenly feeling cold.

'Yeah'

'One of the dog handler's has been killed. Pol...Pol somebody.'

'Polglase. Polly Polglase?'

'That's it. Died in a shooting accident. The other handler, Phil, got wounded during a track that went for fucking miles apparently. Dog pointed but they tracked on and he was hit by Charlie. He's okay. Real fucking mess, mate. Really sorry to put all this shit on you.'

He saw my face and fumbled on for words. 'Jeez, I'm sorry, mate. I'm a driver and 3RAR Trackers said to come and see you if I was over here.'

He waited for a minute while I tried to light another cigarette. I fumbled and dropped it between my feet. I went in the tent and lay down. I put a towel over my face. For some reason I didn't want to look at the light. Polly dead. He loved *The Sun Ain't Gonna Shine Anymore*.

He used to stand in the middle of the hut and mime the words until someone threw a book at him.

Polly. Standing over his bed driving the dog sled, yelling 'Mush!' A shooting accident. Vietnam was the easiest place in the world to have an accident...and die. A loose grenade on webbing. A rifle with the safety catch off, you trip, and the man in front drops dead. A crap in the jungle, walk out through the gun so the sentry can watch you, lose your way... walk back in through another gun...and die. An artillery round drops short, a gunship wobbles as it looses its rockets...and die. A fucking Cobra thinks you're Charlie and blows the shit out of you.

Everyone was a walking accident. Everything around you

was loose and lethal. Then there's the fuckwit who says to the dog handler, *track on...let's see what happens.*

I sank into a depression for days.

SONG BA DAP, PHUOC TUY, JULY 1967 – PART 2

'Get us out. Let us out, we're being stung to bloody death down here!'

The APC commander stuck his head inside. 'Problem down there?'

'Problem? Bloody problem? You've dropped a fuckin' red ants' nest down onto us, cockhead. Open the back. Let us out, for God's sake.'

'Okay, okay. Keep calm and don't move around too much.'

'Don't move? Dear Mother of God is this bloke for real? *OPEN THE FRIGGIN' DOOR.*'

With a whoosh the back ramp lowered and we stumbled and half fell over smashed and shattered trees before falling into two heaps either side of the track. I frantically ripped my shirt off, pulling ants off my chest at the same time as trying to keep Caesar still. Thank heavens his eyes and nose were okay. He could deal with a bite or two on the dick.

I had just got the last two insects off my skin when I became aware of a strange lifting sensation. I was half lying and half sitting up, and the odd movement beneath me felt like I was sitting on an inflating airbed. I spread my legs apart to see what looked like a car inner tube uncoiling beneath me. The delayed shock of the ant poison meant that for a second or two it didn't click that I was sitting on a huge snake.

'You said you wanted to get out, you silly bugger. What are you doin' now?' The APC commander was still pulling the remains of the jungle out of his machine when he was almost flattened by man and dog trying to get back in the APC.

'Shut the bloody door. Vietnam's biggest snake is after me!'

Fergie was coolly pulling his pants back up and brushing ants off the seat. 'It's a python, dork. It'd eat the dog, not you.'

'Yeah, well fuck you too. Python or not it'd take you down in one gulp.'

The APC rewed up, and in a few minutes we reached the enemy bunker system where the trackers were waiting. I took several minutes to examine the ground and the trees and carefully inspected the surrounding bush before I settled down for a brew-up.

Revelation

It was the final two months in Vietnam, and within a fortnight the 4th Battalion Advance Party, along with the replacement dog handlers, would arrive at Nui Dat. We were all uptight, buggered and sweating out the countdown as Short Timers.

You've come the distance and still got your balls intact—and the last thing you need is another operation. Coburg and subsequent ops had squeezed the last reserves of juice out of 2RAR; the grunts were grunting through the tour's endplay with grim faces. The Tet Offensive had been vicious, unexpected, real. It sapped the diggers' humour, shredded bravado, and filled a few church services in the battalion chapels. We didn't want any more deep insertions, camping out in tiger territory.

We hoped like hell there wouldn't be another major operation…so they gave us one.

'Bear Cat! Bloody Bear Cat! They get mortared and rocketed every night in Bear Cat. Anyone told these bastards there's an offensive still on?'

I was throwing my first serious fear fit in the tent at no-one in particular. We were all getting short in country, we were suffering short-timer's syndrome: could we survive a couple more months? Could we avoid major operations and the chance of getting wounded or zapped? I was getting seriously scared.

Fergie was shaming me by busying himself getting the dogs ready for another road convoy north. I decided to quieten down, put on my flak jacket and helmet and grabbed Caesar's lead. I consoled myself with the fact that we weren't getting on a chopper; I couldn't stand the dog going mad again—I'd kill him.

Bear Cat was a large American military complex west of where 2RAR and 3RAR would operate. We were essentially going back to the Operation Coburg area because US Command felt sure another Tet was about to start. We would join the Task Force HQ and remain at Bear Cat until we were called out—if we were called out—by the rifle companies who were stomping through the jungle again looking for the NVA.

The American complex was a dirty, dusty city of low bunkhouses, which were not unlike the old Ingleburn lines, but for the fact they were shielded by sandbagged blast walls. There was a good reason for that. From the little we knew about Bear Cat, home to the 9th Brigade, it was an ocean of choppers and military machinery; one of the huge logistics centres that fuelled and fired the war where a multitude of men were in continuous transit, along with thousands of tons of supplies. It was not among the biggest bases in Vietnam, but it was, we had learned, sizeable enough to attract regular rocket and mortar attacks—even ground probes.

The conversation I was now having was one-sided, like the day I joined Tracking Wing and a red-faced Carter was bawling me out for being hatless. The over-weight, obnoxious, loud American officer had lassoed me as soon as I got off the truck and hauled Caesar and I away from Fergie and Marcus. We had been press-ganged as soon as we alighted. What jobs we were being hit with, fuck knows.

'Chopper control, that's your job for the next few days. Bring 'em in, send 'em out...you know how to operate a 25-set?'

I stood with Caesar on the side of a landing area in the

middle of what looked like the biggest helicopter parking lot in the world. My task was to control multi-millions of dollars in aircraft which would land and take off all day, everyday resupplying the American and Australian forces on operations to the north and east.

I didn't know what to say to the Yank officer who looked like he was going to pat me on the head before he walked away. It occurred to me he hadn't seen the dog I had on a leash next to me—maybe he thought it was my pet and not a war dog at all?

I was shown the ropes by a young GI who was dragging on a cigarette. He looked younger than me, and had a curious southern accent that was hard to get a handle on. It was simple stuff, said he. Basically the pilots of choppers would call me up to say they were on their way, and I was to tell them 'on the raydeeo' the chopper pad in front of me was clear.

'Clear 'em to land, but don't fuckin' do that 'till the one in front's gone, otherwise you'll have an arse-up situation with beaucoup boom-bang when one ploughs into another, uh-huh.' He put the radio handset to his ear and mumbled, 'Watch me, uh-huh.'

I watched dumbfounded. What the hell was I doing here? Where was Fergie?

'Look, this is a bit bloody stupid, mate. You may have sort of noticed I'm a dog handler, I'm a tracker, not a friggin' air controller. Your boss has picked the wrong bloke...'

I was waved to be quiet as the radio hissed to life. Caesar heard the choppers first. Dozens of drones, scores of clattering and whining engines and the slicks of Iroquois appeared over the trees.

The American called one in. It bumped down and was up

and away again as quickly as the soldiers on the other side of the bitumen landing strip had stacked rations and water and backloaded empty jerry cans. In moments my instructor had called another one in, it was gone and then another Huey touched down. So adept was the young air controller he caused virtually no holding pattern around the base. I had little time to pick up tips because Caesar had turned into a frothball, breaking his neck and my arm to get on the choppers.

After half an hour things went silent and I squatted with exhaustion. The soldier looked at his watch.

'Ah'm goin' for a dump, so you can take over, uh-huh?'

'Uh-huh,' I replied and asked him if he could take the dog back to the hut and lock him in.

'We can't put pet dawgs in the sleeping quarters. He'll have to stay here, uh'm afraid, buddy.'

'Yeah, well *buddy*, I've gotta problem. You see this dawg gets sort of funny around choppers and we seem to have a lot of choppers comin' in, uh-uh?'

What the hell was I going to do? Were was Fergie? Where was anyfuckinbody? The Bear Cat bunch had obviously been briefed they were to get an Australian relief radio/air controller. I was now standing like a shag in the middle of a heliport with an animal who had serious psychiatric problems with helicopters. Why was I surprised? This was Vietnam.

The radio was hissing. 'Uh-huh' had gone to the crapper—and certainly wasn't coming back now he had a dopey digger doing his work—and any moment I'd get the call for clearances. I knew radio procedure and how to work the 25-set. I opted for action, grabbed Caesar and tied his leash to my pack and webbing on the ground. I pushed my Armalite through the shoulder straps and bound the leash to the stock. He could run, but not too far.

'Now listen, Caesar!' He was looking skyward. *Take control, Peter, take control. The dog knows, he senses your authority...never a need to be brutal. Arthur Eather, Tracking Wing.*

'Caesar! This is it, mate. We're in the shit. No, *I'm* in the shit. *Please, no more going mad.* The last thing I'll ask of you in Vietnam is please no more chopper madness. Just for me, boy?'

The dog looked at me, straight in the eyes, and there was a flicker of understanding. I really thought for a moment maybe he felt sorry for me. I whispered a prayer he'd got the message and at the same time the radio hiss stopped and an American twang came over the air.

'Bear Cat, Wild Cats seeking clearance, over.'

I grabbed the handset and looked across the strip where men were lounging on boxes of rations. Must be okay to come in.

'Wild Cats, Bear Cat. Clear, over.'

'Bear Cat, Wild Cats. Affirmative, out.'

I looked down at the dog. He was sitting staring across at the loading party. *No one in Trackers is going to believe this,* I thought as the slicks appeared, bobbing like corks on the horizon.

'Please, mate, *please* leave the choppers alone,' I whispered in Caesar's ear and gave the war dog a hug.

The next minutes I could concentrate on nothing else other than stopping 20 choppers rear-ending. They came, landed, they left, and I talked everyone in, shouting into the handset with shoulders turned to the downwash of stinging sand and grit.

Suddenly there was silence and the loading party across the strip was gone. My head was splitting and I was half deaf and shaking from the rush. I had become a chopper air controller.

Smoke, heck, I needed a smoke and a drink. It was when I reached for a water bottle in my webbing, it hit me: 'Where's the dog?'

Caesar was lying next to the webbing, front legs out, studying me. Not a yelp, not a shake; no crazy frantic burst of madness. For a moment I couldn't think straight. Was he all right…gone catatonic?

He sat up, yawned and looked at me. *'All you had to do was ask nicely and I would have done it long ago. You always shouted at me and pulled and twisted my collar. I would have thought by now you'd understand me…'*

It was a day I would remember. I was the fool who learned his lesson. I'd broken his bad habit…nearly a year too late.

'Hey, Aussie, you wanna bone for your dog?'

The Yank was a small, fat, sweating cook who accosted me walking back from day two on the chopper pad. Caesar had been quiet, finding little to explore at the huge sterile Bear Cat complex, and his head shot up at the word 'bone'.

'Hell, yeah, that'd be great. Got two? We got two dogs.'

'No shit, you have two pets hounds up here?' Before I could tell him to fuck off, they're weren't pets, he waved a hand and vanished into the cookhouse.

Marcus and Caesar hadn't had any meat bones since the tour started that I could recall. They were both now wrestling with two massive leg shanks in the shade of our hut. We had put the animals under the hut at night with two bowls of water and instructions to the locals they were not to go near the 'killer-attack' canines from Down Under. Like steaks and fries in the boonies for the soldiers, raw, bloody, fat-covered bones were simple pleasures to the war dogs, who were absorbed in demolishing them for the next two hours.

Top: Resup for Grunts. The author (centre) loading supplies at a fire support base shortly after the TET Offensive was launched in February, 1968.

Bottom: Faces of War. Tracker dog Tiber replaced Cassius after he died from heat exhaustion. Tiber is pictured here with handler Norm Cameron of 7RAR during operations in July 1967, their faces etched with fearful anxiety. (Australian War Memorial/COL/67/552/VN)

Top: Flying High. US choppers carrying Trackers and support infantry in southern Phuoc Tuy province. (R. Moodie)

Bottom: Getting Out. An Australian chopper lands in a jungle clearing to extract the Tracking Team.

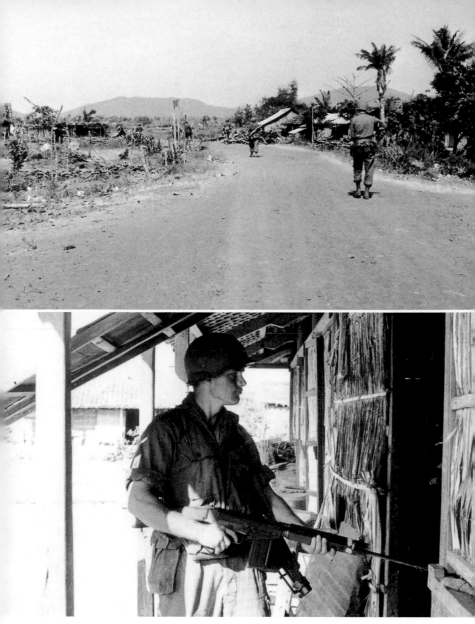

Top: On the Road, Far from Home. Members of the 2nd Battalion patrol a village before a house-to-house search begins.
Bottom: Going In. Tracking Team coverman Les fronts up during a village search.

Above: Wet, Wet, Wet. Thatch, the Tracking Team machine-gunner, soon after falling into a rice paddi field. The Team was following a blood trail at the time the gunner took a dunking. (R. Moodie)

Top: Eyes Wide Open. Tracking Team coverman Les keeps watch during a village search.
Bottom: Time Out. Machine-gunner Thatch practises leaning on his gun during a village search.

Top: She Ain't Heavy. Blue carries an elderly Vietnamese from her home during a village search.

Bottom: Armed and Dangerous. Weapons captured from the enemy and displayed at Nui Dat after the TET Offensive.

Top: The End of the Road. Viet Cong captured after a bunker system search. (R. Moodie)

Bottom: The Sharp End of the War. Viet Cong killed during operations in Phuoc Tuy. (R. Moodie)

Above: Best of Friends. Fergie and Marcus (left) and the author and Caesar in the shade of Nui Dat rubber, in an area where the dogs were kennelled and where they spent time off during operations.

The day before leaving Bear Cat we were determined to go a bit mad. The war was like that, a build-up of pressure, no way to let go unless you could blast something, or someone.

I'd noticed a large swimming pool situated among the living quarters and the sandbagged bays where the choppers were parked. There was a deck running around the pool which was a hell of a size, even for a base this big. I'd seen no-one using it and assumed it was because most of the Yanks were in the field. It was crying out for use, and Fergie and I decided we'd take a late-night dip. I suggested we take the dogs in too.

'They won't like dogs in their pool,' he said. We agreed, bugger it, we'd do it, an after-midnight probe and splash in depth.

'They haven't had a swim since we left Australia. They'll love it,' I explained.

''Specially, Marcus,' Fergie was now convinced, 'he's been hanging out for real water.'

After midnight, not a soul in sight, and we both did a couple of laps. I was backstroking and Fergie was breast-stroking through the black water. 'Jeepers, this is good. Cleanest water in Vietnam and not too much cholrine. I don't like too much chlorine.'

I got out, brought Caesar and Marcus up to the deck and pushed them in. The pair went crazy and took off like they were pursuing a downed duck. With snorts and yelps they climbed on each other's backs then Marcus got out to do his favourite flying bombs.

'What the hell are you fuck-arsin' around at?'

I surfaced with a splutter to be greeted by the big American officer who introduced me to the chopper job. He was standing on the walkway to the pool. 'Wha...?'

'I said what the goddamned hell do you think you're doing?'

'Swimmin',' said Fergie.

The Yank looked so mad I thought he was going to self-destruct and he was still struggling to find words when a black flying mass of fur flew past him and bombed Fergie.

'Is that a friggin' *dog*?'

'Right,' I said, trying to hide Caesar behind me. 'Trackers, we're with the Task Force HQ.'

The officer wheeled and called another soldier over. 'Sergeant, get these men out of the water and make a report.' He stormed off.

I got out and towelled down in front of the sergeant, whose eyes were locked on Marcus who had now heaved himself out of the pool and was giving himself a furious shake. I tried to hose down what was quite obviously a drama to the sensitive men from the 9th Brigade.

'Bit pissed off over a late night swim, wasn't he? Okay, so the dogs are a bit unhealthy, but we're going tomorrow and…'

'I don't think that's what the lootenant is *really* pissed off about, buddy. That's not a swimming pool—it's the base's drinking water.'

We never got any more flak, although we both made sure we kept Caesar and Marcus under cover until the last minute before convoying out of Bear Cat. We agreed we hadn't seen the pair look more full of life in months.

PHUOC TUY, JULY 1967- PART 1

'What's that bloke doing?' Simon jabbed a finger up through the trees.

The Cobra was pure sex—a slab-sided, vicious killing machine, a turbo-charged gunship and the war's latest in technology. The

Vietnam jungle was its proving ground. Here it could place rockets and a sheet of bullets into an enemy concentration, pick off a lone VC fleeing across a paddi, or shred a bunker system...like the one we were searching right now.

The Cobra dipped and weaved and came back over our position, like a cruising shark before a strike. Simon was watching the gunship with a worried look. A worried Simon was a worry. Was he thinking the same as the rest of us—was the Cobra sussing us out as possible Viet Cong? Couldn't our commanders make contact and identify us as friendlies? Could this turn into a very serious fuck-up?

I nudged Les who was doing his best to ignore the threat. 'Anyone know why everyone suddenly has the we-are-stuffed look?'

I had just demolished a can of peaches and fed a packet of biscuits to Caesar. It was now brew-up time during a 10-minute break. Earlier we had located a bunker complex and turned up a ton of rice, plenty of bloodied clothing and two dead enemy, who had been dragged out of a tunnel and moved aside for later burial. There'd be a debate over who got the job of digging graves after our morning tea. APCs were moving up with a team of engineers who would set charges and blow the complex and the rice cache. But right now the Cobra was a big worry.

Blue wandered through just as the gunship thundered in and checked us out again. As it tilted you could clearly see the two-man crew seated one behind the other. 'Hey, stupid, we're Aussies...That mongrel does one more run over and I'm going to lay this on him.' The red-headed gunner extended the legs of his M60.

THE LAST DRY RUN

It had been unseasonably dry for many weeks, with no break evident in the weather. Beating our way through the bush to our night position, you couldn't figure whether it was better to be soaking wet all the time or parched dry and carrying an extra load of water. Asian war was full of shitty options.

We had been attached to Battalion Headquarters (BHQ) for the operation. This meant walking through the jungle to set locations, establishing a defensive perimeter in the bush, waiting, saddling up and walking again like an army of ants creeping north while the rifle companies fanned out east and west across several thousand yards on ambush and search-and-destroy missions. Trackers would be flown out or taken by APC to the rifle companies if the need arose. Or so we thought.

In the meantime it was bush-bash through the northern part of the province on an op that was taking us again near the Mao Tao Secret Zone. The jungle was thick, but with no overhead canopy, so there was no shade. The lower growth was an obnoxious mix of vine, bamboo clumps and thick scrub that closed in around the body almost wrapping a man up in a vicious thorny embrace.

With the dog it was murder. Caesar walked alongside me on the short lead and became as trapped in the undergrowth as I did. After a kilometre of this hell I was going insane with the constant battle to disentangle myself and the dog from clinging lantana. And as much as he tried, Les, walking in front of me, couldn't stop branches and bush flying back into our faces.

With each click covered, water and dehydration also was becoming a growing worry. I tried to keep fluid consumption under control, but every few hundred yards I took a gulp and was acutely aware I had to get water into the dog. The sun hammered down without mercy; no sooner had sweat oozed out of our skin than it was virtually burned out of our shirts. When I placed my hand on Caesar's coat I could feel the heat increasing by the hour. By late afternoon when we stopped to harbour for the night I'd had enough of the dog to last me the rest of the tour. I was wrung out with battling to keep the animal in check and ready to ditch the poor bastard if I could have got away with it.

It took another hour to dig in, trying to scrape shallow weapon pits out around thick roots and rocks, and hack away at ground hard as concrete. The first night we got down no more than 30 centimetres, and tried to make ourselves comfortable with BHQ people and Anti-Tank, who formed the defensive perimeter. There was no time to eat more than crackers and cheese and force-feed a can of meat into Caesar before we collapsed next to the weapon pit and waited for the blackness. I noticed the dog and I already had downed at least three bottles of water. I checked with Fergie next morning—his status wasn't much better.

The Battalion Commanding Officer, Chick Charlesworth, drifted around after breakfast and asked after the dog. He cocked an eyebrow when I mumbled water was a bit of a problem, but gave a reassuring grunt resupplies were planned for next day.

Half an hour later Bill came around looking worried. 'We've got a track, one of the rifle companies has sprung an ambush not far from here.'

Soldiers get gut feelings a stuff-up is in the air, and I'd been in Vietnam long enough to know stuff-ups were part of the landscape. There was a stuff-up, or worse, on its way.

'Let me just get this straight—we've got to *walk* from here to the rifle company to do the track?' I was trying to finish a smoke and pack my gear and the dog's equipment, and absorb what I'd just been told by Bill. 'Walk from here, how far? Oh just a click, just one thousand bloody yards in this shit. Right. How many days have we got to do that? A couple of hours. Right. What shit for brains came up with this bright idea?'

I saw CO Charlesworth watching me from a short distance away, thought of how he knew I liked filling sandbags, and packed up without further comment.

Loaded to the gunwales with full pack and two extra water bottles I scrounged off Blue, I was ready to go. The mini-tracking team was Bill as section leader, Les as coverman and Simon as visual tracker. Four other diggers would act as security on the thousand-metre walk over to the rifle company. I had one last thought yanking Caesar as close into my leg as I could: 'Why couldn't bloody Fergie and Marcus have pulled this one?'

Half an hour away from BHQ and I knew the eight of us were getting into trouble. The jungle was the thickest I'd ever encountered. It wasn't tall timber that climbed hundreds of feet and gave some degree of cover from the sun, but a just-above-head height combination of thick grass, bamboo, thorn and vines wrapped around every bush. There was no trail to follow.

The forward scout was cutting his way with secateurs or pushing and flattening the vegetation in front of him. Every 50 yards he collapsed to get his wind back. The psychological strain of watching for enemy was adding to his growing debilitation. Bill was trying to navigate on a given bearing to the rifle company and trying to keep our location on the map. Each time the scout went down on his knees and held his hand up for a breather and direction check, Bill called up Simon—who was pacing our distance with a sheep counter—to help with the map-reading. Making matters worse for Bill, there were no identifiable topographical features—no clearings, no creek lines, no rising or falling ground. He had an extra aerial photo map which was no great help—it showed grid squares of unbroken light green. We could be 100 yards off the bearing and be none the wiser.

I lay flat on my back, resting on 60 pounds of pack. I was panting, pulling in air that seemed to come straight out of an oven. Caesar stood next to me, his tongue quivering. I unclipped his mug and he slurped up half a cup of water.

'Easy, boy, take it easy as you can.'

Les knelt next to me. 'I'm going up the front to help the scout,' he said. 'Its gonna take two of us working at it to get through this stuff.' Les had to roll on his stomach and push himself up to stand, such was the weight on the little guy's back.

It never failed to impress me how men under such conditions could keep going; somewhere down inside the soldier there was the mental toughness that overcame the physical decrepitude. Exhausted as you felt, you could still dig a weapon pit at night. Physically buggered as he was, the scout never lost the ability to cover his arcs for sign of enemy. And there always seemed the compassion to help another who was as shagged as you. So Les was going to assist the point man without being asked. He could have hung back and let someone else do the hard yards.

With the coverman and scout working at the coalface, we advanced a little faster in the next two hours. But water, or lack of it, was now becoming an obsession. I kept shaking my bottles and calculating how much I had left. Bill used the 25-set to raise the rifle company and give them our locstat and check their grid reference. The news wasn't good. After a few minutes consultation with Simon he reported: 'We've got 500 yards to do, but we are at least 200 yards off the bearing. We've got to swing to get back on.'

Amid grunts and 'fucks' we struggled to our feet and fought through thorn, bamboo and the interminable high grass again. Clouds of dust and pollen rose and choked nose and mouth, and I fought every step to keep the dog in close. When my rifle barrel wasn't stuck on a vine, Caesar's leather lead had become entangled around bamboo stalks. Under my breath I cursed the dog, the bush and myself. I stumbled, fell, became throttled on an overhang or sapped precious energy fighting to loosen my pack from thorny scrub. It was impossible to move in silence; the wheezing and whistling of men struggling for air and crackle and snap of bush would alert VC 100 yards away.

Two hours or more and we were physically and mentally shot, when suddenly the radio hissed, the rifle platoon was alerting us we were close. Next minute we lurched into the rifle platoon's position.

A soldier looked up at me from his lunch of sausages and biscuits. 'Where the fuck you blokes bin? You look like shit that's dried in the sun too long.'

Caesar lay on his side panting, and I couldn't summon the energy to unhook my pack. I lay like a capsized turtle and looked around. The atmosphere in the rifle platoon's location was eerie; there was a silence which had been punctuated only by the arrival of the trackers and our support group, some down on all fours dry-puking through the exertion. Simon was standing with his pack at his feet, wiping his face with a sweat-rag, and Bill was sitting against a tree, head back and arms outstretched in a posture of crucifixion. The scout who had contended with the horrible bush was lying so still I thought for a tick he was dead.

The rifle platoon was spread out in pairs near trees, brewing or munching biscuits. Infantrymen never expended unnecessary energy: if you can sit instead of stand, lie down instead of sit, do it. In tiger country, with the constant threat of VC walking into you, there was silence, communication in whispers, no clink or clunk of equipment, and eyes were locked on the surrounding bush. Out from the platoon single sentries—or listening posts—were posted, with the Australians stationary for more than a couple of hours.

The platoon commander, a tall looey who still believed his men should have their faces covered with camouflage grease, looked like an apparition from a bad dream—comical and dangerous—while he talked quietly with Bill.

I ran my hands over Caesar and gave him another small drink. There was no question he was stuffed, still panting furiously from the battle with the bush and me during the long walk in. I felt a pang of guilt I may have been a bit rough with him while trying to control his walk through the bad stuff. I also asked myself if the exhausted animal was up to tracking. I knew I had no petrol left in the tank.

'Okay, up and let's go,' Bill shouldered his pack with a grunt and pointed out through the trees. 'Simon, do a check and see what sign we have.'

The big visual tracker spat (where the hell did he get the spit from?) and hoisted his pack like he'd been for a walk in the park. I still couldn't stand up. Les still had his eyes closed and was leaning with one shoulder against a tree, still as a shop window dummy.

The ambush site was a small foot-track intersection. One track led down to a dry creek, the other branched and meandered away through thick, low growth comprising thousands of stunted trees. No-one was wounded in the killing ground, no blood, no equipment dropped, but the platoon was certain at least five, well-armed Main Force Viet Cong had wandered in and fled before the lethal Claymore mines were triggered.

I unstrapped the tracking harness, barely able to bend down to do it, and looked at the dog. I was worried as hell Caesar wouldn't work, he had a glazed expression. We needed a half-hour more to recover; we weren't going to get it.

Come on, let's do it. I'm ready. Caesar dipped his head and took the harness. I gave him another quick drink.

'Pete, for God's sake be careful with the water, the bloody rifle blokes have got fuck all left, either.' I could see Bill was concerned.

Simon gave me the thumbs up with a sort of 'okay, I'll keep some back for the dog' look.

Les closed up behind me and lifted his SLR to a ready position. 'Ready when you are.'

A hundred yards and I was on my knees with the heat, exhaustion and thirst. The dog was heaving, every part of his body shuddering with exertion. But he hadn't missed a beat. He switched and cast looking for scent, found it, tracked on, lost the smell, cast in a circle as I dropped the lead to get through the bush, stopped to wait for me, and head down, tracked on.

I couldn't believe he still had it in him. More, as each

minute passed he seemed to be working harder, locked onto the enemy scent, and was even picking up speed. Not unexpectedly, I soon got the hand signal from Les to stop, and Bill and Simon caught up with me.

The corporal was scarcely able to speak. 'Jesus, you're setting a pace. The rifle company boys are whacked. Hold for a few minutes.'

While I struggled to get another water bottle out, Bill went back to check his map with the looey. I rubbed Caesar's head and checked his heaving body. 'You're a bloody marvel. How you doin' it?' Caesar sat and stared into the trees.

Simon walked forward of me with Les covering him and carefully examined the ground. I couldn't spot a single sign left by fleeing men. The visual tracker, though, with a superbly trained eye for spoor, was seeing everything. He gave thumbs up. 'We're right on...watch for a point,' he hissed at me.

The next half-hour I was part in dream, part on the track of the Viet Cong. It was past midafternoon and the heat was still unbearable, with the scent trail winding in and out of thick scrub on no definable pathway. Caesar's tension on the tracking trace was consistent, he was picking up smells all the way while I tried to keep my head up and rifle at the ready.

The dog jerked, lifted his head and his ears shot up. It all happened in a just a heartbeat. I skidded along the ground and knelt next to the dog. I heard Les softly swear and he pulled the SLR up to his shoulder. Silence. Nothing. Not the shrill of bird or rustle in the dry bush. I could only hear myself gasping and Caesar panting.

Putting my finger across my lips I whispered to Les and Bill, 'That's a point. Close, must be close.'

I pushed Caesar under an overhang and felt the taste of

metal ooze into my mouth. Jesus, I needed water. I slipped the water bottle off my belt. Empty. The one next to it was empty. Slide off my pack and pull another one out. Quarter full. Give it to the dog.

Studying the territory ahead told me nothing: a small clearing, dull coloured bush, still those low trees and burning bright light reflected back. Not a shadow, just stark brown and light green. A certainty came over me, an almost spiritual emotion: don't step out into that clearing, you will be shot.

'We can't go on, we've got a problem,' Bill breathed into my ear.

'We're out of gun range, got no artillery cover anymore.'

The 105s at the closest fire support base had been following our progress, and we had gradually tracked out of range. With a heavy contact we would be stuffed for artillery support. We had effectively slipped off the radar. Naked. The correct decision was to go back.

Simon squatted near me and looked at the ground. 'There's another problem,' he said. 'No bastard's got any water left and they're not choppering any in with Charlie this bloody close.'

I told Bill and the looey again the enemy were straight to our front and the platoon commander agonised over the advice. The platoon leader in him said go forward and engage the enemy, but his Forward Observer artillery adviser was nudging him to slip back into gun range.

I took the harness from the dog and scratched in my pack for the last remaining full water bottle. I was so dry I could hardly speak, and kept seeing bright lights in front of my eyes. Simon and Les filled a mug and gave it to Caesar. The dog gulped it down and coughed half of it back up.

'Shit, Les, I hope he's not going to fall over on me.' The

coverman pushed my pack on my back and we stumbled into our withdrawal.

Less than 30 minutes later we all collapsed again while the platoon put in a defensive perimeter for the night. Water— no-one spoke of the unspeakable while we cleared small sleeping spots.

Water. Water from a plastic water bottle, tainted and lukewarm. Water from a stagnant stream, layers of green slime; scoop the scum aside and drink it down. Water in a jerry can, off-loaded from a chopper in a clearing or lugged by APC across parched paddis. Collapse to your knees and guzzle it straight from the spout.

In Vietnam's dry season few things focused the mind like a water bottle running low and another 10 kilometres to walk. You could do days without food resup, but not without water. Travelling with a rifle platoon, I saw a forward scout cutting a trail drop with what sounded like a hiss of escaping air. The priority was to get him out and to hospital fast. They medivaced him, and he just survived. He hadn't consumed enough water.

In the dark I came awake and a moon was up. Caesar was sitting up and looking out into the blackness. His ears were up and his head switched left and right like he was watching a tennis match.

I fought down the sick feeling in my gut. What was the bastard looking at? What could he see that I couldn't? 'Stop that you silly bugger,' I whispered in his ear, but he pulled away and froze, head forward sucking up air scent. I knew what he knew. The enemy were still out there. I didn't want to think it but I was certain we had been followed…and we were going to be hit. I put my arm around the dog and we waited for the moon to sink and the sun to rise.

Before first light we should all have been lying on our guts, rifle and eyes front, instead I was fumbling through my pack and webbing checking if any of the eight bottles had any water in them. Nothing but half of one canteen left.

The sun came up like a fireball, and I got the first good look at my arms and hands. There wasn't a square inch of exposed flesh on me that wasn't covered in rents, tears, scratches and dry blood. Yesterday had been a hell of a day. What about today with no water and—

The explosion behind us sent dirt and shattered timber up into the air in a cloud of black smoke. Immediately an M60 went into overdrive, then single barks and *braats* of SLRs and M16s.

'Contact!' Shouts, yells and we all rolled back onto our stomachs.

Silence. Bill and Simon crawled over to the platoon commander, who was telling his company commander on the radio we had hit the shit. Minutes passed with nothing. Then there was another bang, but this time from a distance some hundreds of yards away. Then rifle and automatic fire.

Everyone asked the eternal diggers' question, 'What the hell is going on?' I held Caesar down close to me and watched my front. Les was only yards away doing the same. Next minute the instruction came down the line, 'get up and piss off, now.'

Half run, half stagger we bush-bashed away from the contact.

It was a command-detonated mine the VC had pushed up near us at night and blew it just after first light. No-one hit on our side, but worse news was another rifle platoon had hit a big group of Main Force Viet Cong only a click away. We had come up against something sizeable—Main Force

Charlie. They had wised up to tracking teams, knew a dog would be brought in after the ambush. They then took off at high speed and waited for us to come after them. We backed off eventually, so they followed us and first light hit us from the rear. Simultaneously, they had hit the rifle platoon one click east. Even my limited knowledge of enemy tactics told me this was planned, premeditated to suck the Australian rifle company into VC territory, a long way from gun support. Correctly, the Viet Cong figured a reinforcement unit would take hours to get up to us. Choppers? Gunships support? Sure, but damn risky judging by the size of the VC force. Packin' death time again.

I glanced down at the dog while we humped through the bush: 'You clever arse dick, you knew all the time the Nogs were out there crawling about in the dark.' He looked up at me, tongue nearly down to his feet, '*Told you, but you won't listen.*'

'Our situation is quite critical. We have two men down with possible heatstroke, a tracking dog not in the best shape and no water at all.' I was close enough to hear the radio message. Caesar was lying on his side breathing short bursts, and I could barely move without the lights flicking across my eyes. My stomach and legs were cramping, and when I stood my vision blurred. I had a King Kong-size headache. Everyone else was in the same boat—no water, and we couldn't eat because we couldn't drink and there was no shade from the incessant heat frying us in the low bush.

There was more radio traffic, much mumbling over maps and the order was given—get up and move.

The enemy hadn't appeared, but no question they were following us, maybe hoping to wear us down. I guessed the tail-end charlies in the platoon, those pulling up the rear in the single file of retreating soldiers, were shitting bricks. A grim-faced Simon had his M79 blunderbuss, his rifle and personal magnum at the ready. He looked at me. 'Taking your mind off sex yet, Pete?'

I made a mental note as soon as we were hit to stand behind the best-armed man in the outfit. A hundred yards later we stopped and the war dog collapsed in a panting fit. Les waved his bush hat over the dog while I trickled my last drop of water into a steel canteen and induced Caesar to drink it.

'There's a clearing ahead and they're bringing APCs from Route 328 over with water.' Bill gave us the news then struggled to his feet. He looked at me. 'We're gonna make it. Just a little more humping.'

The last few hundred yards through the clinging, grasping, thorns and vines was hell. It was unreal; I was floating—no pain, just the constant visions of cool running water, condensation beading on cans of VB, cloudburst and freezing monsoonal rain, buckets of it, sliding into deep blue pools of water, standing under showers and gulping down jets of the liquid.

There was a sudden burst of fire across to the east again. 'Heavy contact,' Les wheezed. 'Keep going or we'll get it next.'

Every man retreated into his own world of move and survive. Keep moving towards the carriers where there were men and firepower. I stumbled, staggered, tripped and fell. I yanked and pulled at the dog, swearing at him with anger and frustration. Caesar just became more entangled and trapped in the bush, at one stage he looked like he was caught in a cargo net of vines and tree branches. It took me precious minutes to unhook and encourage him to soldier on.

Behind me Les was coughing and hawking, in front of me Simon was trying to carve a tunnel for me and the dog to move through. We told ourselves, *get through this and you'll get through anything*.

God, I whispered, I promise I'll never be bad again.

Through the hum in my ears I heard a growl and grunt, a revving engine. 'Carriers!'

The platoon halted to check we hadn't been followed, a typical Noggie trick—tail us to the APCs and open up while our guard was down. During the minute's halt Caesar flopped on his stomach…and then crashed sideways.

'Shit, shit, shit,' I dropped my pack and lifted him. He was panting furiously, two veins either side of his eyes had swelled and his tongue was a vicious red.

'Les, Les, Simon! Hell, I'm losing my dog!'

I picked him up, God knows how I had the strength, and stumbled out to the closest APC. I knew Caesar's internal organs were probably cooking. Like Cassius, he would be dead in maybe a few minutes.

The carrier commander saw me coming and dropped the back of his tank. Two men pulled jerry cans out and we splashed water over the dog. By now soldiers were staggering and stumbling and falling over themselves to get at the water, despite shouts from the platoon medic, 'Don't drink too quickly!'

PHUOC TUY, JULY 1967 – PART 2

'I don't like this one little bit—he's going to have a go.' Simon and Blue exchanged words and everyone started to stand up. Searching the bunker system was all but forgotten. There were now urgent exchanges going out over the radio with attempts being made to call off the Cobra. It didn't seem to be working. Then there came the sound of what sounded like a bedsheet being ripped in half, a tearing rent and the trees overhead whipped and buckled.

'Mini-guns! He's opened up! Get the hell down!' Les yelled, looking for shelter. Every other man hit the ground. One place to go, just one place to get below ground level and that was into an enemy bunker. It was distasteful, unthinkable, maybe dangerous. You just didn't go into these holes that led into tunnels that took you into God knows what underground. I stepped down into the closest tunnel entrance and pulled Caesar in. He braced both front feet and looked at me with what was obviously 'No bloody way, Jose'.

'It's down here or get shot to pieces—now in. Now!' Nothing in tracking training had prepared us for this. The smell was possibly repellent to the dog. Maybe Caesar suffered claustrophobia, I know I did. Both my arms around the war dog, and we tumbled back just as the Cobra made another sweep. The last words I heard before backing into the tunnel were, 'Check fire! Tell him to check fire!'

I crouched in the tunnel holding onto a dog who was shaking with the canine equivalent of a nervous breakdown. 'Stop shaking, I'm as scared as you,' I whispered into his ear. Snatches of the past conversation with the Airborne troops came back. 'They're surrounded by savage little bamboo-spikes, pits, command-detonated mines with beaucoup bolts, nuts and nails. And there's a lot of other fuckin' stuff yo' an' us ain't never even dreamed of. Gooks are creative little fuckers when it comes to killin'.'

Outside now there was only silence. No Cobra. I wondered for a minute if everyone had taken off and left us behind. So this is how they lived and fought. Sitting and crouching in here waiting for the shells, the bombs, the bullets to pass over, then crawl out and go at us again.

There were the growls and clunks of APCs coming up through the forest. The engineers had arrived.

GOING HOME

I had arrived in Vietnam with Caesar as a 19-year-old freshmeat, green, naive teenager. A year behind us, and I had physically deteriorated. My body weight had dropped so much I was rake-thin. My wrists stuck out of my shirt cuffs like thin bamboo shoots, my neck was scrawny and there were visible rings of red from dust and mud that were almost impossible to scrub out. My lower legs and lower arms as well as my bony hips were covered in sores that resisted all modern medicine's ointments and creams. Circles of red—some breed of Asian ringworm—covered my crotch area and my feet and toes had long been taken over by tinea and a version of Vietnam footrot. Black rings were a permanent feature around my eyes.

Leaning against the cut-down 44-gallon drum we used as a dog bath, I studied the dog; the friend who had been a close companion for the past year. He had recovered from his brush with heat stroke and seemed his perky self. But watching me through the arcmesh of his cage, I could tell Caesar had suffered effects of the year-long tour. He had matured, become quieter, and at times even introverted. He was leaner, his ribs showed through, and he'd had some bark knocked off him here and there. His mental state was a lot harder to determine.

Despite the trials the war dog had endured, through all the misery and fear he had always treated me like a close mate. We had comforted each other in some odd man-and-dog fashion. Now the unthinkable was happening. Each hour, day, week and month had brought us closer to the trauma of separation. I was leaving the war. Caesar was staying.

I never really knew how much he meant to me, how I had come to love him until I nearly lost him. 'We've been through a lot and you never let me down. I hope I never let you down, either,' I said to him.

Can't we stay together now we've been through all this? Who will look after me when you've gone? Take me where you're going and we can still always be with each other.

Seven days and a wake-up. The battalion prepared to leave, and the two replacement dog handlers had arrived from Australia with the advance party. We briefed them on what seemed an impossible mission: to learn the ways of our two tracking dogs—and how to track—in a week. I found a piece of suitably thick vegetation on the side of Nui Dat hill, laid a couple of 200-metre tracks. I walked behind the new handler, trying to explain what a point was.

At night we discussed the absurdity of what we were doing, cramming the basics of dog handling in Vietnam; what had taken us more than a year to achieve in Australia we tried to pass on in a week. We blamed the stupidity of the Army: why the hell didn't the new battalion, 4RAR, bring its own dogs so we could take our two home? What we felt more was what we couldn't—wouldn't—discuss, the fact Caesar and Marcus were staying in Vietnam. I still fed and walked Caesar each night, with the new man in tow. The dog didn't seem to know time was short.

I couldn't get into the swing of RTA, the booze-ups in the canteen, the relief of men realising they'd made it. From our battalion strength of about 1000, twenty-eight 2RAR men didn't make it, killed in action, and another 122 had been wounded. We figured we'd killed nearly 200 enemy, by body count, and the Vietnam War's checks and balances were all done on body count.

I packed my steel trunk and loaded the stereo gear I'd bought on rest and recreation into a container that would be shipped home on the HMAS *Sydney* with us. The rest of the time I lay on my cot and read, polished up my boots for the mandatory march we'd have on RTA, and raked leaves around the tent. I was going into another depression.

Day of departure.

I was shaved and dressed in new greens, had my hold-all packed, and sat on my stretcher looking at Fergie. We'd agreed I'd go first, spend a few minutes with Caesar, come back, and he'd go and say his farewells to Marcus.

Fergie was sitting in a chair studying the light bulb. 'Hell, this is hard, mate. I knew it would be, but hell, not this bad. Why, why the hell? Just why…?'

I made some coffee over a hexamine block. 'Norm told me before they went home they offered to pay $2000 to take the dogs back, quarantine bills and all that stuff. They were knocked back and told the dogs had to stay and keep working. I don't think a dog can do more than a year on the trot over here. Jeepers, we couldn't.'

I stepped out of the tent and turned towards Company HQ, crossed the road and saw the kennels a short distance in front. I forced each step, head down. The other handler had stayed in his tent, recognising I wanted this time alone.

Caesar saw me coming and jumped up on the arcmesh, while Marcus was in his favourite position, on his back, legs in the air snoring. I walked up to the fence and stuck my hand in for a playful bite.

'I gotta go, you gotta stay, that's the bloody way they run this war. You've got a new boss, but I don't ever want you to forget me, I won't ever forget you…'

I stepped back and Marcus woke up. Both dogs looked at me.

They're leaving us, old dog, you know that don't you. Going home and we're staying here.

The tears started to well up and Caesar picked his bowl up in his mouth. I turned and walked straight back to the road. I heard the bowl hit the concrete floor and fought with every fibre in my body the urge to look back. I felt a ton of lead fall from my chest straight down through my stomach.

In the tent I started to hyperventilate and hung my head while Simon, Blue and Bob looked in. Fergie got up and took the long walk up to the kennels. I shoved my hand over my mouth when I felt sobs coming on. I didn't want to make a spectacle of myself.

'Let it go, let it go. We'll never forget the buggers,' Blue patted me on the back.

It was June 1, we flew out on the Chinooks and 4RAR flew in. We hardly brushed shoulders on the swap over.

LOOKING BACK

July 1968. The sun chased me through the car's rear window along the Pacific Highway. I had taken four weeks leave, bought a '65 HD Holden, and was still living in that excitement you get with your first set of wheels.

I had passed Bulli, the tall forest where it all started, and had now swung inland towards Appin, past the scrawny scrubbiness of Helensburgh where we'd swore and grunted through the 10-milers. Right turn at the Appin intersection and on to the small village of Campbelltown. The sun was dropping when I sighted the tall stand of gum trees signalling I was approaching the Infantry Training Centre. Creedence Clearwater came on the car radio, *Run Through The Jungle*. The main gates to Bardia Barracks loomed up, left turn, guardhouse on the left, post office on the right. Swing hard right down the shady avenue to Battle Wing. I parked behind the orderly room and lugged my bag down to the Tracking Wing huts. I found an empty room and tossed my gear on the bed. No-one around on Sunday night and I should have unpacked, but there was something I needed to do.

I walked quickly down to the war dog kennels just as the last light was going. A soldier appeared and asked me who I was. I told him I'd been posted to Tracking Wing and I was one of his new dog handling instructors.

'You had a dog in Vietnam, then? What was his name?'

I didn't answer him, instead I made my way to the side of the vet room where the graduates were attached to the wall. Cassius, Justin, Caesar, Marcus, Julian, Janus, Tiberius, Milo and Trajan headed the list with the others who had been posted to battalions but not gone overseas. I had to look at the names to confirm where I'd been for the past year. Did it really happen? I was in that curious twilight zone, a sort of mental dislocation. Turning from the shed I saw a dozen pairs of eyes looking at me. The new guys, all black shiny coats, faces alert. For just a stupid moment I thought I saw a dog up on the fence, one ear flopping, and felt a lump forming in my throat.

I had a smoke near the obstacle course and walked back up through the trees. For me the war dogs' kennels would be home for the next two years.

Norm from 7RAR and Bob, my former Team Commander at 2RAR, joined the Tracking Wing after their leave, and we formed the nucleus of the training component. The unit was in the throes of training a whole new batch of handlers and visual trackers. In Vietnam the war went on.

They speak of the arrogance of youth, the years when the juice flowed, the righteousness, the egos and immortality; characteristics, I discovered, which protected and shielded the young veteran from the aftermath of war. So, I had a positive attitude to training and instruction, no post-combat stress, but there was just the occasional blip which came in the form of flashback.

It was when I thought of Caesar I had problems; guilt and remembrance. Not a word came back from Vietnam on the dogs—if they were working, if they were alive. Typical Army, its lack of communication and the need-to-know mentality.

I trekked behind the handlers while we worked the five- and 10-milers, watched them conducting obedience with a whole new generation of tracking dogs. For a moment I thought I saw a ragamuffin looking up at the sky for a bird, or having his compulsory leak before putting his nose down to business.

At Bulli a bunch of vets had constructed a Viet Cong camp for the purposes of training, a benefit Caesar and I had never had. It was complete with bunkers, spiderholes and thatched huts. The first time I saw that camp I had a bad flash, a momentary wince and intake of breath. The only thing missing, I told the handlers, was the smell. You could never recreate the smell. I remember I sat once on a bunker like the fake one at Bulli, smoked a Salem, drank cold milk and abused a Korean cameraman. Marvin Gaye was on the radio, but I couldn't recall the song. Walking up to that Bulli camp I swore sometimes I felt the jag and jerk on the tracking lead...

There was always the rain at Bulli. It sometimes bucketed down in the forest, and I remembered Damian and Arthur Eather, doubled in pain with his ulcer, threatening to charge anyone who threw the errant dog over the escarpment. I had sat in the rain once with a rifle company, a shared misery, with a plastic sheet over my head, and Caesar huddled in trying to push me out. We caught the run-off the plastic and drank the cool, clean water. The rain hammered so loudly on the plastic hootchie you couldn't talk.

I saw a butterfly at Helensburgh during a five-mile track with a new dog, and suddenly there was a body in front of me covered in white butterflies.

Vietnam, months after a homecoming, was images. The glimpse of understanding at Bear Cat during the chopper landings; the look back in danger yards away from a mine in the Long Green. Not all uncomfortable images, just disquieting, unwelcome, for a moment. And, there was an occasional jab of pain and emptiness when I lay on my bed and heard *The Sun Ain't Gonna Shine Anymore*...

Two years almost to the week after marching into Tracking Wing and my promotion to Corporal, I was posted out to 3RAR. They made me a section commander with Anti-Tank/Trackers. It took a while to sink in that 3RAR was in its final stages of training for a tour of duty. I was going back to Vietnam. A moment of dread turned to resignation, which turned to anticipation. Maybe, just maybe, I'd see *that* bloody dog again.

NUI DAT, 1968

I was going out with Thatch on night TAOR patrol-ambush, along with a gaggle of misfits selected from Administration and Support Companies. Selection was random; Thatch and I drew the proverbial short straw. It was a pain in the arse, an overnighter, sitting under a bush two clicks outside the wire, watching for the enemy to come along. There'd be 10 of us, a fighting section of drivers, clerks, hygiene people and a corporal in charge. Everyone at Task Force did a TAOR at some time; every man on the base was expected to be a soldier, know his contact drills, know elementary fieldcraft, go outside the wire.

Thatch and I ate early and made our way down to the rifle company exit near the perimeter wire. We met the others going out and did a quick equipment check. I took a Claymore mine and carried a belt of link for Thatch's M60. The corporal was a driver from some transport unit, and I noticed straight away by the look of his webbing that he hadn't done a lot of bush work—it didn't fit properly, and hung loosely on even his overweight body. He studied me while I was checking my magazines and came over.

'You the dog handler with Trackers?'

'Yeah, me and the gunner are from Tracking Team.'

'I want you to scout for us. Bein' as you ain't got your dog, reckon you can do that?'

I thought we've got a smart arse here, and didn't bother to answer him, but my ears pricked up when I heard him mumble to another digger about 'not getting one yet'. I sidled up to the soldier and asked what that was all about.

'He wants to kill a VC before he goes home and thinks he'll get one this time.'

I went straight to Thatch. 'We've got a fuckin' John Wayne here, wants to kill a Noggie, and wants to get one tonight.'

'Well, so much for a quiet nap in the bloody scrub.' Thatch knew as well as I did these types existed in Vietnam. He wanted something to talk about when he got home, how he'd been under fire and seen action with the real enemy, spin war stories. In this case his only VC was going to be peasant caught out wandering through Line Alpha after curfew. How switched on was this bloke? I hoped like hell he'd worked out his map properly and didn't have us wandering into a local village in the dark.

It took an age to walk through the massive perimeter wires, and I moved to the lead as the sun was beginning to set. We had a fair walk ahead of us to the predetermined ambush site. It was a strange feeling, walking free of the dog, almost liberating, and I could give my all to watching and picking my way through the low bush.

I had studied the map and knew which way to go without consulting the shitwit section commander who was patrolling shoulder hunched and rifle swinging left and right like the actor Vic Morrow in *Combat*. I found a broken-down fenceline and used that to keep my bearings. I figured it about another 200 yards to the ambush, which would be on a foot trail leading from a disused paddi to some old rubber.

Everything was turning grey, no shadow in the minutes before sunset; the sort of look the world gets when you lose perspective slightly, a kind of night blindness. Suddenly there was a clicking of fingers and a low whistle behind me. I turned, and the corporal was motioning to me.

191

'Shit, you missed the bloody Noggie back there,' he hissed into my ear.

'What bloody Noggie? You mean a VC?'

'Yeah, yeah, a Gook.'

Australians never referred to the enemy as Gooks, and I thought 'he's been with a bunch of GIs in a Vung Tau bar at some time'. I quickly knelt and adopted a fire position. I scanned 360 degrees. I must have been going blind. I could never have walked past a Charlie?

Thatch was now up with us. 'Wassup?'

'A VC over there, look. He's having a smoke sitting on the fence,' finger madly jabbing into the gloom at the fenceline.

Thatch looked at me then slowly peered around and back at me with a wink.

'Shit! You're right. Reckon he's got a bloody AK too.'

'I knew I'd get one, I fuckin' knew I'd get one eventually.' Our section commander was almost having an orgasm over a ghost, and I was inwardly begging Thatch not to play along, but the big gunner was going to have some fun.

'Shall I give the bugger half a belt, uh?'

'Jesus, yeah, shoot the little bastard.'

Before I could protest Thatch was down on one knee the M60 was up and half a belt of 7.62mm ripped into the old fence, tracers bounced brightly over the paddi and the remaining patrol dived for fire positions, yelling, 'Contact!'

The corporal was beside himself with the taste of action and did what I'd never seen anyone do in Vietnam: he stood, held his rifle to the front and screamed, 'Charge!'

Thatch immediately knew he had overplayed his hand and mumbled, 'Oops, fuck', before running and going to ground in the old paddi field.

'Great manoeuvre, Thatch. What's next?' I snorted at the gunner, meanwhile terrified at the thought of the next move from our deranged leader. Too late, he already had the radio handset and was checking his code to call in mortars.

Enough. I scrambled over. 'Listen, mate, there's nobody here. Call up for mortar support and you'll have the whole friggin' Task Force on alert.'

His eyes were spinning in his head. 'Reckon we musta wounded him. He'll probably be back.'

Thatch appreciated the need to restore sanity. 'Yeah, I'd say you're right. Why don't we go ahead with the ambush and catch him. Good idea, huh?'

'Good idea.' The corporal got to his feet, and we hastily set up an ambush position in bushes on the track.

I crawled in next to Thatch and dropped the link next to the gun. 'Shit, every bastard in Nui Dat, and we get a gung-ho to lead us.'

The gunner was slumped over his M60, shaking and fighting back laughter.

'S'allright, that idiot won't sleep all night watching for his Charlie, so we can have a good zonk.'

RETURN PERFORMANCE

Luscombe Field, February 1971. Wallaby Airlines Caribou flight from Saigon, and I was back.

Five years 1ATF had been here, and the only change on the face of it was that the rubber trees had attracted a heavier coat of red Nui Dat dust. So had the tents; still sagging and as drained of energy as the men who had just walked out of them. From where I sat on the cot it was a case of massive deja vu; the bug-speckled light bulb, the rupturing sandbags, the leaves hanging in the flysheet.

Doesn't anyone ever clean up before they go?

I was now a section commander, a leader of 10 men—no, make that eight. No unit in the history of the Vietnam War had ever been up to strength.

I expected the worst. I had missed Caesar by just a few months. He had gone, pensioned off and sent to Saigon. I tried to wrangle a trip to Saigon to find what sort of life he had retired to. It never worked out, and soon I had other things to worry about.

We were out on operations immediately. One boot placed in front of the other, across the paddies, through the bamboo and into the aquarium zone under double canopy. The constants were everywhere: slicks of choppers, the crash of the 105s, fire bases, digging in, ambush, and night harbour where the blackness was still so intense you could breathe it.

We only did eight months of the scheduled 12 and the Australian Government pulled the pin.

The official record showed 519 Australians dead and nearly 2500 thousand wounded, for others a lifetime of scars from poisoning and post–combat stress. The end of this war couldn't come fast enough for me.

It was a stint on Operation Overlord that drove in the final nail. Bravo Company had taken a huge bunker system and brought what the Americans called a shitstorm down on the VC. We followed the Australian Centurion tanks into thick jungle where a resupply chopper had been shot down by enemy fire. The sight of the burnt-out shell of the helicopter hanging in the trees like a gutted shark got us all uptight, and the fact all the crew was dead had everyone spitting chips. We had to stay several hours in the stinking, wet hole and from where I took up a fire position I noticed a Centurion tank had moved through and squashed a dead Viet Cong into the mud. Curiously his hand and wrist protruded from the slime, almost an appeal to be pulled from his final resting place. To me it was something more: the hand was a last gesture of defiance in a war he had already won.

Twenty years after I first toured Vietnam I talked my former 3RAR platoon sergeant, Allyn McCulloch, into coming with me to Sydney for The Welcome Home Parade.

On 3 October 1987 we walked over the hill to the Domain and there were 25 000 Vietnam veterans gathered to march and where, maybe, the celebration and acceptance would purge forever the ghosts of war. It certainly did. At the end of the parade I felt a relief and unloading I could never have imagined: I cried, straightened myself up and then caught a taxi to a reunion of the 2RAR Trackers.

All but a few had made it. Now middle-aged men, fighting the flab, worrying about retirement and battered and bruised after banging into too many of life's sharp edges. We stood locked in debate, sank glasses, jugs and buckets of beer. Argued, laughed, joked and remembered.

Bob, Blue, Fergie, Donny and others whose names I struggled to remember sat down at the table staring at the mysterious metallic disc— shiny, worn and slightly bent with a clip ring through a small hole.

Where the hell had it come from? Turning it into the light we could just read the worn engraving:

AUST MIL FORCE D6N03 CAESAR.

He was a mongrel from death row. He was saved and conscripted to serve his country. He asked for nothing but was asked to give everything. To the soldier the Vietnam War was like all wars—mateship and loss. Australians died in Vietnam, but no man was abandoned there. Caesar and his mates were. Dogs go with men into war because they have no choice.

But all the horrors aside, I comforted myself with the thought that to Caesar the war was his chance to experience his great adventure.

EPILOGUE

The second tour of Vietnam, I now admit, led to a dysfunctional post-service life. I nursed grudges and hated authority. If every Vietnam veteran returned from the war with his own private demons, I certainly had mine. And as the years drifted by I thought more often about the dog I had known. A friend left behind, passed on like a pair of old boots.

Eventually it happened to us all: we lost our protection, the resilience of our youth.

After Vietnam, the men who fought with the Combat Trackers were scattered to the winds, back to lives they had left before the war. But some were changed men. After 12 months staring into the face of the Beast, they were withdrawn, unsure, uncommunicative, wandering and adrift— brain-fucked. This was a condition that was to afflict many for more than 30 years.

One of the major differences between vets from the World Wars and Vietnam was the absence of what we today call safety nets and networks. Only half a dozen diggers I had served with in 2RAR lived in South Australia. I never saw them post-war. There were no reunions at the local RSL, no Sunday barbecue with half a dozen ex-comrades. And counselling centres—when you did feel a wire had shaken loose—were non-existent.

When I returned from 'Nam I recall disembarking from the HMAS *Sydney* in Brisbane—2RAR's home base—and flying to Adelaide where I then caught a taxi home to find my mother and father asleep in bed. It was a strange way to come home from war. But there were reasons, my mother explained: 'They didn't want us to know when you boys were returning because those protest people might do something.'

After Vietnam, my years were spent nursing shame and embarrassment over my war service. Talking about active service was like farting at the dinner table. So I got shit-faced at the dinner table instead and, occasionally threw a ranting and raving fit. It was, I learned much later, the beginning of war neurosis. It was called shellshock in the Great War, battle fatigue in World War II. But for Vietnam, we eventually conjured up a user-friendly, psycho-babble medical term which perfectly fitted the Vietnam veteran. It categorised him without, presumably, humiliating him; it entitled him to counselling and tranquillisers, but didn't quite certify him for a padded cell. It was 'post-traumatic stress disorder' (PTSD), and it covered every complaint from rashes and war 'flashbacks' to the troppo digger standing on the front lawn with a rifle at the ready daring the cops to shoot him. Vets soon figured the best way to deal with PTSD was either to drown it with grog, or seek help. I soldiered on, ignoring the condition, until a friendly GP told me to stop drinking or die. I stopped drinking.

Today I suffer minor effects: I resent anybody in authority, I can't stand incompetents, and I shout a lot. I also experience the insidious nature of Vietnam flashbacks in bizarre ways—like walks in the bush with family and friends where they admire the flora and fauna and I admire possible fire positions, distances to fallen logs or high ground, calculating how many seconds it would take Caesar and I to get there in a contact. Loopy? Sure, but it makes perfect sense to me, and I still do it today. This was known in Army parlance as being 'switched on'. And on operations I was always switched on; hours of concentration, nerves taut like fencing wire, zinging away all day, most days. After Vietnam a good many combatants never 'switched off', exacerbating other, more serious war traumas.

Then there is smell association, where I will dig in the garden, roll over a pile of decaying leaves and that smell will surge up my nostrils. Zip! Back to the jungle, where each boot turned over those leaves and the combining stench of leaf-decaying mould, which had been percolating for 100 years, was released and wafted upwards. This is hardly life-threatening stuff, but it is nasty, unwelcome, disquieting. And it hovers around me most days, waiting for the signal to be invited in.

I also lost a few close friends after the war. One of them was an old school mate who said, after I came back: 'Forget the war, everyone else has.' To this day I resent him for saying that.

The upside to my war service is…well, there is no upside. I've got three medals, loads of old black-and-white photos and colour slides, and a letter from the government in 1998, which says:

A grateful nation thanks Peter Haran for contributing to Australia's effort in the Vietnam War.

Funny about that—in the early 1960s the government said there wasn't a war. I still smile when I look at it with John Howard's signature on the bottom, reckoning it must have been held up in the mail for 30 years.

What happened to the other guys from Trackers? I rang around and found a few and we met in Brisbane on Anzac Day in 1997 to celebrate the 30th anniversary of our departure for war.

Big Simon, the visual tracker, was called up in 1965. He was from an established pastoral family in the Riverina. Simon was one of those nashos who extended after his obligatory two years, and he went on to another tour of

Vietnam, where he was a member of the 9RAR tracking team. When he left the Army in 1970 he worked with the Freedom of Information Department in the government and moved his family to Canberra. Simon, with his wife and four daughters, is now in semi-retirement but is still very active in the martial arts. He is a qualified national referee in judo, and the gentle giant will be part of the Australian technical support staff for our judo contingent at the Sydney Olympics.

Bob, my former team commander, was originally from Queensland, but settled in Campbelltown, New South Wales on his discharge from service in 1970. Bob joined the Federal Police and at the time of writing is a detective with the force. He has three daughters.

Thatch, the machine-gunner, settled in Darwin after his two years of national service. He married and had four children, all girls. Thatch used to drive trucks before the war, but now works for the Northern Territory Lands, Planning and Environment Department as a technical services manager.

Red-headed Blue went back home to Kurri Kurri on the New South Wales central coast after discharge. He worked as a leading hand in an aluminium processing plant until he was diagnosed with severe PTSD in 1996. Blue, who has two children, remains an active worker with Vietnam veterans and is a campaigner for their rights and welfare.

Fergie left the Army after the 1967-68 tour of Vietnam, but rejoined and returned to the war with 2RAR on their second tour in 1970, where he was reunited with tracking dog Marcus. After his discharge, the former dog handler settled in his home town of Redcliffe, Queensland. He was diagnosed with severe PTSD and now lives on a war pension.

My close comrades aside, I always wondered about other diggers I had shared a miserable moment with—the men from the rifle companies, the grunts, like those blown up and fucked over in the Long Green.

The Vietnam veterans I knew never asked from their country more than they were entitled to. That included some degree of compassion when they sought treatment for wounds and scar tissue that they had brought home. And they asked for a chance to live a normal life. Was that really so much to ask?

BRISBANE RSL, ANZAC DAY, 1997

I was waiting for the ex-Trackers to roll up as part of the 2RAR 30-year reunion. I had rocked up an hour early and was sipping a Coke when I noticed a man walk through the main entrance.

He wore faded jeans, a checked shirt and his hair stuck up at a hundred different angles. He was unshaven and had a wild look, like he'd slept on the beach for the past five years. I wondered if he'd be chipped over his dress code, but then thought, heck if he's a returned serviceman, he's got as much right here as the next bloke.

He spotted me, walked over, pulled up a chair and nodded, 'You here for the 2RAR reunion?'

I nodded back and bought him a beer, then asked who he was with in Vietnam and how he'd been for the past 30 years.

'Rifle company and absolutely no bloody good at all. I told them when I got back I was fucked; after all that Song Rai shit.'

Song Rai was a sizeable river in Phuoc Tuy province and it was frequented by the VC. I was dying to ask him if he'd been in the Long Green with Trackers when we got the shit blown out of us, but before I could ask he was back on the Song Rai.

'I was scouting and first across the river by myself when bloody Charlie gives us a big hello. Fucking bang, I'm down with rounds flying over my head and the rest of the blokes are on the other side of the river. Oh, I says, this is real fucking nice, is anybody going to, like, get me fucking back please?' He looked at me and drank and refilled his glass.

'You know what the first thing you do is when you're going to die?' I looked at him, waiting, trying to think what did I do. Piss down my leg, I think.

The digger whispered to me: 'You call for your mother. I ate dirt flat on my guts and called for my mother for nearly a bloody hour 'till they got me back.'

He went silent but was still churning the war over in his head, all the while moving his bottom jaw back and forwards in agitation.

'I got a Harley when I came home, and went up and down the New South Wales north coast for years. Got married. Fuck that, couldn't get it right, and pissed her off. I drank piss all day and every time I told the VA (Department of Veteran Affairs) I was stuffed in the head they pissed me off, too.'

The ex-scout eventually bought a caravan and lived in the bush with his 'special plants', his SKS automatic rifle and his Bundaberg Rum. Within years he had gone fully feral, hit the wall, and opted to kill himself.

'I said bugger them all, no bastard's goin' to listen so I turned all the gas rings on and had a Bundy.'

Ready for the Big Sleep, the old soldier decided to have one last smoke. He rolled a cigarette and flicked his Zippo.

'Fuck, you wanna see what a load of gas and light does to a wooden caravan? I was lyin' on my arse in the bush and my mobile home was spread out for a hundred fuckin' yards. Couldn't get that right, so I called the cops out with a few bursts on the SKS. Next minute, flashing lights, wallopers in flak jackets everywhere and I got a real belting. "Right", some bastard says, "It's the psych ward for you, mate." No worries, I tells them, that's where I wanted to go all the bloody time. I reckoned at last I got it right.'

The old soldier laughed, and bought another beer. This time his leg was twitching from the knee down and his jaw was working backwards and forwards ten to the dozen.

'What I was going to ask you was whether you were in the Long Green?' I said cautiously. He shot a dagger-look at me.

'I'm telling the story, right?' I went silent and he went on.

'I'm in psych ward, and I says I ain't staying here unless me bike comes with me. They bloody reckon they can't have a Harley in hospital, but after I start making threatening sounds like taking some bastard in a white coat out, they bring the Harley in and wrap it in plastic in the hall. Great, I have a rest and they assesses me. Yep, I'm a full-blown nut. Pension please? Ta very much. And they says I can go tomorrow.'

'I'm out mate. Tear the plastic off the bike and fucking, whoompa, straight down the passageway and straight through the flyscreen door.'

I am still leaning forward picturing the veteran making his last break for freedom like a triumphant Easy Rider, but now he's looking around the RSL lounge, face vacant and rolling another cigarette. I prompt him.

'Yeah, so how did things go after that?'

He suddenly looked back. 'Bloody useless. The bastards didn't tell me I was on the first floor. Ten minutes after I'm out of hospital I'm in again with a fractured pelvis.'

He slumped forward, elbows resting on his knees, spitting bits of loose tobacco while I fought to keep a straight face.

'You know, after bloody Vietnam, I can't get any bloody thing right.'

Appendix

Dog Tags

July 1970. Three years after his first live track in Vietnam, Caesar was loaded into the back of a Caribou aircraft at Luscombe Field. With the canine veteran was Rod Purcell, a handler trained at Ingleburn during my two years there as an instructor. Their destination was Saigon.

Caesar was suffering from heartworm and was battered and bruised, not only by his war service—three times the duration a soldier was expected to do in combat—but also by dogfights with kennel rival, Juno.

Purcell and Caesar arrived in Saigon and were driven to a French villa set in cool, shaded gardens and surrounded by a high stone wall. This was Caesar's last flight as a war dog. He was now retired and became the property of the Air Attache at the British Embassy. He was handed over with his dog tag still around his neck.

Purcell and fellow handler Arthur Taylor were part of the 7RAR Tracking Team. They had worked Caesar and tracking dog Juno during 7RAR's 1970-71 tour of Vietnam. Very shortly after Caesar's retirement, Juno was handed over to the Australian Embassy in Saigon. The 7th Battalion was soon to be relieved by 3RAR, the unit I was returning with, and had three dogs to dispose of before we arrived—Caesar, Juno and Tiber. Tiber had been the replacement for Cassius after he died in 1967. Along with Marcus and Caesar, Tiber had been the longest serving Australian war dog in the Vietnam War.

But Tiber had suffered the canine equivalent of shellshock

while serving with 1RAR during a vicious and prolonged ground assault at Fire Support Base Coral in Bien Hoa province in 1968. The animal had been semi-retired, whiling away his days with working dogs Caesar and Juno in the shade of Nui Dat rubber. He was given to the Military Police at the Task Force Base as a mascot and pet.

The life and times of the 11 Australian war dogs in Vietnam is confusing. The simple reason for this is that infantry battalions rotated every 12 months and the dog, or dogs, were simply passed on to relieving units. For example, Norm and Tom passed Justin and Tiber on to 1RAR in 1968. Fergie and I handed our dogs over to 4RAR in the same year. More dogs arrived, some as 'reos'—reinforcements—and the rotation system continued. By the time the war had wound down most dogs had been donated or given away, and the survivors were burnt-out shells waiting to be put out to pasture.

What did happen to the war dogs left in Vietnam? After extensive reading and a score of interviews with former trackers and dog handlers, nothing is certain, no-one is sure and there is little agreement on exact times of transfer to various battalions and the final move to retirement.

There is one relieving aspect to this whole disgraceful mess, and that is my worst fears were not realised—no dogs were 'put down', and every effort was made to give the dogs to good homes. The animals' disposal would have been a highly sensitive issue; obviously, the Australian Military Command did not want to give—or be seen to give— Australian war dogs to Vietnamese nationals.

There was likely a good public relations reason for this, and it was directly connected to the death of dog handler Garry 'Polly' Polglase, who was killed in Phuoc Tuy province on 13 April 1968.

Polglase's dog, Julian, had been trained by a young handler called Bob Pearson, who stayed at Tracking Wing, Ingleburn when Polglase marched out to 3RAR with Julian in 1967. Pearson was too young for active service at the time. Before leaving for Vietnam, Polglase took his pre-embarkation leave and went home...taking Julian with him. This was strictly forbidden, but such was Polly's rebellious nature. His family, including his mother, became very attached to the tracking dog, and that fondness became a catalyst to almost a national controversy when Polglase was killed. The family, led by a determined, grief-stricken mum, lobbied the Army and politicians to bring Julian home in memory of the dead son. The Minister for Army intervened and promises were made, then broken. The cost of quarantine would have been about $650 at the time but, more to the point, Julian was a 'serving member' and so had to soldier on. The ink splashed around during the debate would not have been lost on the Army Command, who would soon be facing the vexing question of the war dogs' disposal, either after burn out or military withdrawal. Inquiries showed the cost factor of returning the dogs to Australia was irrelevant, as Mrs Polglase had raised enough money in public donations to bring all the dogs home. The debate eventually fizzled out. The public forgot that dogs were serving in Vietnam as well as soldiers.

In an ironic twist to the Polly Polglase tragedy, Julian's original trainer, Bob Pearson, arrived with 9RAR at Nui Dat in 1968 and took over the dog when 3RAR departed. A search through Central Army Records Office (CARO) has thrown no new light on the war dogs' demise. Many soldiers who worked with tracking dogs felt a year was long enough for a war dog in Vietnam; at the most two years, and the animal would be suffering. He was exposed to every bug and infestation known to man, he worked as hard as any combatant, and on more than one occasion was exposed to horrendous battle conditions, including artillery fire, mortar bombardment and rocket assault. There was no complaining, no whingeing. They all worked at call, travelled up the point, and many a soldier will testify that their lives depended on the war dog's willingness and ability.

Using information from battalion yearbooks, and reports from the trackers themselves, here is an outline of each war dog's service:

CAESAR: Originally trained and handled in Australia by Phil Little, Casesar was taken over by Peter Haran and was posted to Vietnam with the 2RAR combat tracking team. He was initially handed over to 4RAR. He later served with 5RAR and 9RAR in 1969-70, and was then posted to 7RAR. Caesar was retired to the British Embassy in Saigon in July 1970.

CASSIUS: Arrived in Vietnam in 1967 with 7RAR and his handler was Norm Cameron. The dog was a former guide dog for the blind. He died from heat exhaustion at Vung Tau.

JANUS: This dog arrived in Vietnam with 3RAR, and his original handler was Phil Moore. Janus was an exceptional tracking dog who followed an enemy party for up to several miles after a ground assault at a fire base on 17 February 1968. The dog pointed at the enemy, but was ordered on by the follow-up group commander. Moore was shot and wounded just minutes later. During a subsequent track, Moore was again wounded. Janus was rotated to 9RAR and possibly transferred to 8RAR. It is probable he was one of the dogs left at 3RAR in 1971 and his disposal is unclear.

JULIAN: His original trainer was Bob Pearson, but he was taken to Vietnam by Garry Polglase with 3RAR. The dog was taken over by handler Wally Barnett after Polglase was killed in a shooting accident on 13 April 1968. Julian was then transferred to 9RAR, where he was taken over by his original trainer, Bob Pearson. Julian was later posted to 8RAR, where his handler was Len Taylor, and later still to 7RAR and 3RAR. During war service his hearing deteriorated and he became quite sick. It is possible he was given away to an American school in Saigon in 1971.

JUNO: This reinforcement dog arrived in-country in 1969 or 1970, and was attached to 5RAR, replacing sick dog Justin. He was transferred from 7RAR to 3RAR, but it is unclear what became of him after 3RAR left in 1971.

JUSTIN: Arrived in Vietnam with 7RAR. His handler was Tom Blackhurst, who was killed on 17 April 1971 while on his second tour of Vietnam with the Australian Army Training Team. Justin was rotated to 1RAR and suffered war neurosis during the battle at Fire Support Base Coral. He later transferred to 5RAR, where his handler was Dennis Rowlands, and on retirement in January 1970 was given to the manager of the Chartered Bank in Saigon.

MARCIAN: This reinforcement dog saw war service with 4RAR and his handler was Dave Nelson. He was given to the Consular British Embassy in Saigon in November 1971, the same month Milo was given to the Chartered Bank.

MARCUS: Trained and handled by Denis Ferguson in 2RAR in 1967-68. Marcus, bred from a former Australian champion, was owned by the former Governor of New South Wales, Sir Roden Cutler. He was rotated through battalions back to 2RAR (second tour) and, remarkably, was taken over by Denis Ferguson his original 2RAR handler in 1970. 'I saw a tear in his eye when I returned after two years,' Denis recalled after arriving for his second tour of Vietnam. Marcus was transferred to 4RAR in 1971, at which time his sight was failing. His disposal is unknown.

MILO: Served with 4RAR in 1968. The dog was donated in Australia by a family from Hornsby, New South Wales. His handler was Barry McDonald. Milo served with 4RAR, was transferred to 6RAR in 1969, and may have been posted to 2RAR in 1970. He was reportedly given to the assistant manager of the Chartered Bank in Saigon in November 1971.

TIBER: This dog replaced Cassius in 7RAR in 1968 and his handler was Norm Cameron. The dog was later posted to 1RAR, and was involved in action at FSPB Coral with Justin. Tiber fled during the height of a ground attack and returned the following day. He suffered severe shellshock. Following his service with 1RAR and 7RAR's second tour, where his handler was Bill Palmer, he was given to the 1ATF Military Police as a mascot/pet (in 1970).

TRAJAN: This dog served with 4RAR in 1968–69. His first handler cannot be located. The dog went with Milo to 6RAR in 1969–70, where his handler was Bruce Williams. Trajan's whereabouts after that are unknown.

Dogs trained and left in Australia after postings to battalions include Nero and Remus (3RAR), and Cicero and Rufus (9RAR). During 1RAR's second tour in 1968, the unit employed two American Forces scout dogs. The German shepherds were not successful, and one was killed in a contact.

For further information on the author of *Trackers*, unpublished photographs, and a tribute to National Servicemen, visit the website www.vietnam-crossfire.com.

Glossary

General

1, 2, 3, etc, RAR: Battalions of the Royal Australian Regiment (infantry).

25-set: AN/PRC 25 VHF man-portable radio set.

1ATF: First Australian Task Force, based at Nui Dat.

A4: Any Army charge sheet brought against a soldier for a military offence.

AVFN Radio: American Armed Forces radio station in Saigon.

Beaucoup: French/Vietnamese word used to describe 'a lot' or 'many'.

Betel juice: Red juice secreted from betel nut when chewed.

Black boy: Australian plant with long stem growing in sandy areas.

Casevac: Casualty evacuation by dustoff helicopter.

Charlie: The Viet Cong, also known as **Victor Charlie** or **VC**.

Click: 1000 metres.

Cross, the: Kings Cross, a red-light district in Sydney.

Digger: Australian soldier.

Dustoff: Evacuation of the wounded by special helicopter.

FO: Forward artillery observer who travelled with infantry troops to direct gun fire.

FSPB or FSB: A fire support base, or fire base, established as an artillery position in the field during operations.

Grunt: Affectionate term for infantry soldier.

Harbour: Defensive position adopted by a section or platoon of infantry usually during a night stop on operations.

KIA: Killed in action.

Line Alpha: Distance up to 4000 metres from the task force base inside which Vietnamese were not permitted.

Locstat: Location status, map reference indicating where a company or platoon was located in the field.

Looey: Lieutenant.

Medivac: Medical evacuation from the field through illness.

Monty: A certainty.

Nasho: National Service person.

NCO: Non-commissioned officer.

Nog: Derogatory term used by Australian troops to describe the enemy. American equivalent: **Gook**.

NVA: North Vietnamese Army regular troops.

OC: Officer commanding a major unit.

Piquet: Sentry duty.

Punji pit: Pit containing sharpened stakes.

RAP: Regimental Aid Post.

Recce: Reconnaissance to survey or probe an area for enemy presence.

RSL: Returned Serviceman's League.

RTA: Return to Australia.

Sapper: A soldier from the Royal Australian Engineers (RAE).

SAS: Special Air Service.

Sitrep: Situation report by radio from soldiers in the field.

Slick: Group of helicopters.

Stick: Group of men ready to board helicopters.

Stokes litter: Special stretcher used to winch or lift a casualty into a helicopter.

TAOR: Tactical area of responsibility.

Toke: Joint, marijuana cigarette.

Tracer: A round that provides a red or green glow at the rear to enable soldiers to see the round's trajectory.

VC: Viet Cong, described phonetically as Victor Charlie in radio transmissions.

Web belt: A belt from which a soldier hangs water bottles and ammunition pouches.

WIA: Wounded in action.

Zippo: Cigarette lighter, ubiquitous in the war.

WEAPONRY—GUNS

155: A large self-propelled gun used in fire support of troops.

AK-47: Soviet or Chinese 7.62mm automatic assault rifle used by VC/NVA forces.

Armalite: Lightweight 5.56mm US automatic rifle which became standard issue to American forces. Also known as the AR-15, and later the M16 rifle.

Bandolier: A shoulder-carried ammunition pouch.

Canister: Anti-personnel artillery or tank round containing flechette or chopped steel rod.

Claymore mine: Command-detonated explosive device loaded with small steel balls used to defend a position or ambush the enemy.

Colt AR-15: See Armalite.

Flechette: An individual dart from either a flechette artillery or tank anti-personnel round. Each round contains several thousand individual flechettes and is designed to break up a massed infantry assault.

GPMG: General purpose machine-gun (the M60). Standard 7.62mm belt-fed weapon carried by an infantry section.

Howitzer, or 105: Artillery piece used by Australians as heavy fire support weapon. Fired a 105mm shell.

Jumping jack: See M16 AP mine.

M16 AP mine: An anti-personnel fragmentation mine, also known as 'jumping jack'.

M60: See GPMG.

M72: Lightweight, shoulder-supported, 66mm HEAT (high explosive anti-tank) rocket launcher.

M79: Infantry section weapon which fired a 40mm high-explosive grenade.

Owen machine carbine: 9mm submachine-gun produced in Australia.

RPG: Rocket-propelled grenade carried by the enemy, fired from a shoulder-supported launcher.

SKS automatic rifle: A Soviet or Chinese 7.62mm self-loading rifle.

SLR: 7.62mm semi-automatic self-loading rifle, was the standard infantry weapon issued to Australian troops.

Transport

APC: Armored Personnel Carrier used as a troop carrier, fitted with heavy calibre machine-guns. Also known as **tracks** or just **carriers**.

B52, or B52 Stratofortress: A heavy US strategic bomber.

Bird dog: Small fixed-wing reconnaissance aircraft used to spot for ground-attack aircraft.

Caribou: Twin-engined light transport aircraft.

Centurian tank: Australia's main battle tank during the Vietnam War.

Cheyenne: Medium-sized high-speed observation helicopter.

Chinook: Large twin-rotor helicopter (CH-47).

Coyote: Small high-speed reconnaissance helicopter made by Hughes Corporation.

Hercules C-130: Long-range heavy transport aircraft with four engines.

Huey: Iroquois helicopter, Bell model UH-1H, used as a multi-purpose aircraft in Vietnam.

Iroquois: See **Huey**.

Kiowa: Light observation helicopter similar to the Jet Ranger made by Bell.

Lamboretta: Three-wheeled motorbike used as a taxi.

Sioux: A light utility helicopter.

Sky Crane: Large helicopter made by Sikorsky, used to lift and carry heavy loads.

Starlifter: American long-range heavy transport aircraft with jet engines.